EARTHQUAKE

The Earth series traces the historical significance and cultural history of natural phenomena. Written by experts who are passionate about their subject, titles in the series bring together science, art, literature, mythology, religion and popular culture, exploring and explaining the planet we inhabit in new and exciting ways.

Series editor: Daniel Allen

In the same series
Volcano James Hamilton
Waterfall Brian J. Hudson
Fire Stephen J. Pyne
Earthquake Andrew Robinson

Earthquake

Andrew Robinson

REAKTION BOOKS

In memory of my parents, who experienced the
Loma Prieta earthquake in California in 1989

Published by
Reaktion Books Ltd
33 Great Sutton Street
London EC1V 0DX, UK
www.reaktionbooks.co.uk

First published 2012

Copyright © Andrew Robinson 2012

Printed and bound in China

British Library Cataloguing in Publication Data
Robinson, Andrew, 1957-
    Earthquake : nature and culture. – (The Earth)
    1. Earthquakes. 2. Earthquakes – Social aspects.
    I. Title II. Series
    551.2'2-dc23

ISBN 978 1 78023 027 6

CONTENTS

1 Earth-shattering Events

Not long after midnight on an ordinary evening in late February 2008, I had an uncanny seismic experience. I had just finished writing a review for the scientific journal *Nature* of an intriguing book by a Californian seismologist with the attention-grabbing title *Apocalypse: Earthquakes, Archaeology, and the Wrath of God*. While editing my draft, I felt the floor in my fourth-floor flat in London shift almost imperceptibly for a second or two. My partner joked that it must be an earthquake, but I couldn't believe it. In four or five decades I had never knowingly witnessed a British earthquake. Perhaps the vibration had been caused by a London Underground train passing not far away from our early Victorian square. I forgot about it and went to bed.

The following morning, however, the BBC radio news bulletin confirmed that there really had been an earthquake, at 12.56 a.m. The British Geological Survey had monitored the event as having occurred at a depth of 5 kilometres (about 3 miles), with its epicentre in the county of Lincolnshire, around 200 kilometres (125 miles) roughly north of London, and with a potentially destructive magnitude of 5.2. According to the survey's records it had been the biggest earthquake in the United Kingdom since 1984; in other words, for nearly a quarter of a century.

One serious injury was reported: a student in his attic bedroom was hit on the pelvis by a falling chunk of chimney stack. Many houses close to the epicentre suffered damage, chiefly to chimneys, roofs and garden walls. And a lot of people were rudely awoken from sleep and became alarmed enough to go into the street; local emergency services and the British Geological Survey were inundated with calls. A resident of nearby Scunthorpe told a national newspaper: 'My whole house shook like it was going to fall over and it felt as if the whole roof was coming off. I thought a tree had been thrown into the roof by a tornado or something.' Another witness, further away from the epicentre to the south, in Northampton, also thought that his house was coming down. He added: 'I knew it was an earthquake straight away. It was as strong as I have ever felt anywhere, and I lived on the west coast of America for four years.' A third person, resident on the nearby east coast, commented that the tremor was 'much stronger' than one he had experienced in Los Angeles.[1]

Every year in Britain some 200 minor tremors are recorded by seismographs. A magnitude-4 earthquake occurs every two or three years on average; a magnitude-5 quake every ten years on average. In 1931 there was a quake of magnitude 6.1 – the largest British earthquake measured by seismologists to date. As a rule 90 per cent of these tremors go undetected by the public. Those that are noticed – like the 5.2-magnitude earthquake on 27 February 2008 – are rapidly forgotten. To most people earthquakes and England would appear to have little connection, and British earthquakes seem a topic that offers hardly anything of interest to a writer compared with the almost apocalyptic earthquakes that strike places such as California and Alaska, Chile and Peru, Mexico and the Caribbean islands, North Africa, Portugal and Italy, Turkey and Iran, Pakistan and India, Indonesia, New Zealand, China and Japan, where violent shaking of the earth has devastated towns and cities and killed millions of people in the modern period. (In China alone earthquakes have claimed 13 million lives since records began three millennia ago, of whom 830,000 died in one mega-disaster in 1556.) Yet the facts of the historical record show that such complacency and indifference towards British earthquakes are unwarranted.

An authoritative study of the subject, *A History of British Earthquakes* by a mathematician, Charles Davison, published by Cambridge University Press in 1924 just before the advent of modern seismography, lists 1,190 earthquakes that the author was able to authenticate. For the period up to AD 1000 Davison was compelled by lack of evidence to consider a rare, two-volume compilation published in London in 1749 by a Sheffield physician and Fellow of the Royal Society, Dr Thomas Short, entitled *A General Chronological History of the Air, Weather, Seasons, Meteors, etc.* Short noted that he had spent sixteen years collecting his 'scraps of histories', but sadly he elected to provide virtually no details of his sources.[2] His first report of a British earthquake, dated AD 103, refers to an unnamed 'city' in a western English county, Somersetshire, which was supposedly 'swallowed up, name and all' – a disaster that seems highly improbable, and was dismissed by Davison. A later report in Short's book, dated 811, states that an earthquake 'destroyed' St Andrews in Scotland ('most of the town and 1,400 people') – another claim dismissed by Davison and others as a tall story.[3]

But after leaving behind Short's catalogue, Davison's sources become more reliable, that is, from about 1000 onwards, and give examples of some authentic British earthquakes. In 1114, during a violent earthquake in England – which coincided with one in Italy – the unfinished walls of a new Lincolnshire church at Croyland (modern name Crowland) 'gave way, and the south wall was cracked in so many places that the carpenters were obliged to shore it up with timbers till the roof was raised'.[4] In 1248 the vaulted roof of the celebrated medieval cathedral at Wells in Somerset was thrown down by an earthquake. In 1580, in London, a boy and a girl died during an earthquake under masonry falling from Christ's Church Hospital, St Paul's Cathedral was slightly damaged and the great bell in the Palace of Westminster was set ringing. At Dover part of the white cliffs fell into the English Channel along with a portion of the castle wall. In 1692 a violent shock with its probable focus in Brabant (what is now the Netherlands and Belgium) made people in London 'greatly affrighted', according to a letter written soon after by the diarist John Evelyn, whose son lived in central London. Evelyn himself, then in Surrey, felt only a minor tremor.[5]

During 1750, which became known as the 'year of earthquakes', several areas of the country were shaken. In London four

shocks occurred in February and March, the fourth of which
was centred two or three miles north of London Bridge, lasted
for between five and six seconds and caused great stones to fall
from the new spire of Westminster Abbey. This was followed
by a tremor on 20 March. Londoners became so alarmed by a
madman's prediction of a future shock on 7–8 April that thousands of them chose to spend the night out of doors, either in
tents in Hyde Park, in their carriages or simply in the open. Some
women even had 'earthquake gowns' made to keep them warm
while sitting outside on this unique occasion, noted the aristo-
cratic Horace Walpole in an amused letter to a friend on 7 April.
Those who could afford it – some members of the nobility and
the gentry – left London altogether: 'within these three days
730 coaches have been counted passing Hyde Park Corner, with
whole parties removing into the country', reported a sceptical
Walpole.[6] Nothing happened on the predicted day (though in
June there was a 'loud report like that of a cannon' at London
and Norwich, without any tremor).[7] But the earthquakes proved
a boon to certain clergymen, including the evangelist John
Wesley, who prayed from their pulpits that sinful Londoners
would repent and avert God's wrath. Moreover, many Fellows of

Earthquake alarm in
London, April 1750,
engraving.

56   *The Great English Earthquake*

TERRIBLE EARTHQUAKE IN ESSEX.

Great Alarm & Damage to Property at Colchester.

LANGENHOE CHURCH DESTROYED

Wyvenhoe, Mersea, and other Parishes Wrecked.

Not within living memory has Colchester been thrown into such a state of excitement, consternation, and panic, as it was soon after nine o'clock on Tuesday morning, when the town was visited by a fearful and most appalling earthquake, which will remain in the recollection of those who experienced it to their dying day. Everything was peaceful and quiet early on in the morning, no fresh atmospheric change from the last few days, with the exception of a slight elevation of temperature, being experienced to indicate in any way the approach of a visitation of this nature, from which England happily has been very free, and has had little or no cause to anticipate anything of the kind either in years gone by or at this more immediate period. The awful event occurred between a quarter and twenty minutes past nine o'clock, coming without the slightest warning, and lasting from five to ten seconds, but in that short period of time, an amount of damage was done to property which it will take weeks to set right, and in some cases the destruction is irreparable. From one end of the town to the other the ground was convulsed, and if a spectator could have taken a bird's eye view of the Borough, the effect would have been much the same as a sea wave, the ground upheaving and lowering by means of that gigantic power pent up beneath the earth's crust. The general impression appears to be that the ground and the houses with it was lifted up, shaken two or three times in a manner that made the stoutest heart quake, and the bravest to cow with fear, and then subside, disappearing with a kind of final shake or jerk, and then all was over. No noise like the rumbling sound of artillery in the distance, no crash similar to that of a thunderbolt, or the roaring of the boiling ocean, as one expects to hear accompanying a shock of this nature, but there was simply a sort of low rumbling sound, caused as it were more by the crashing and shaking of the houses than anything else. Not a house in the Borough escaped the mighty influence, clocks stopped, bells were set a-ringing, furniture displaced, pictures dislodged from the walls, vases and ornaments overturned, and no end of damage of a more serious character was done in the space of a few seconds.

'Terrible Earthquake in Essex', the Great English earthquake, 1884.

Havoc in Colchester, the Great English earthquake, 1884, magazine illustration.

the Royal Society, most notably John Michell at Cambridge University, were at last provoked to begin research into earthquakes. By the end of 1750 almost 50 articles and letters on the subject had been read before the Royal Society, which were promptly published as an appendix to its *Philosophical Transactions*. Davison notes that the serious study of British earthquakes may be said to date from this time.

Then, at 9.18 a.m. on 22 April 1884, came the so-called Great English earthquake, the most damaging quake of all, which wrecked houses and toppled churches in and around the ancient Roman town of Colchester in the coastal county of Essex while pitching the engine driver of the waiting Colchester to London 9.20 a.m. express train out of his cab onto the station platform. It also rattled nearby London. In the Houses of Parliament, within the Palace of Westminster, puzzled MPs were 'stopped in their tracks, jolted against walls, or felt papers and briefcases jerked from their hands'.[8] Officials were immediately dispatched to investigate the possibility that there had been a Guy Fawkes-style explosion in the cellars of the palace, perhaps set off by the notorious Dynamiters who were at that time being prosecuted by the police for their anarchist activities. The British earthquake of 1884 lasted for perhaps five seconds (like

that of March 1750) according to a reliable eyewitness near the epicentre, a professional sailor who was no stranger to earthquakes in other lands. Had it lasted a few seconds longer, noted a sober report in a local Essex newspaper four days after the dramatic disturbances, 'there is little doubt that the countryside would have been completely destroyed and the loss of life would have been incalculable'.[9]

England's greatest writer, William Shakespeare, was clearly alive to the reality of local earthquakes in the sixteenth century judging from a number of references to them in his works. In *King Henry IV Part I* Hotspur declares:

Diseased nature oftentimes breaks forth
In strange eruptions, oft the teeming earth
Is with a kind of colic pinch'd and vex'd
By the imprisoning of unruly wind
Within her womb, which for enlargement striving
Shakes the old beldam earth, and topples down
Steeples and moss-grown towers (III, i).

Three significant English earthquakes – in London in 1580, in Canterbury in 1580 and near York in 1581 – are known to have occurred during Shakespeare's early youth (he was born in 1564). One of them is thought to have been the source of a topical reference in his play *Romeo and Juliet*, when Juliet's nurse remembers an unforgettable day:

'Tis since the earthquake now eleven years,
And she was wean'd – I shall never forget it –
Of all the days of the year upon that day (I, iii).

The most likely candidate is the London earthquake of 1580, which caused a real stir, as we know. Some Shakespeare scholars have therefore dated the original composition of *Romeo and Juliet* to 1591, eleven years after the earthquake. Others, however, prefer 1596, the year before the play's first publication.

Earthquake depicted in
The Illustrated Bartsch,
before 1500, woodcut.

All of this is not to suggest that British earthquakes have any global significance. Indeed, they will hardly rate another mention in this book. But their very existence over many centuries serves to illustrate the truth that no part of the earth is entirely free from the effects of earthquakes – not even stolid Britain.

On the other side of the planet, by contrast, on the Pacific 'Ring of Fire', jittery Japan is, of course, an authentic earthquake nation – perhaps the quintessential one, given that most of the country has long been severely affected by shaking and the Japanese have made earthquakes a part of their government and culture. Seismologists have determined that today's Japan receives nearly 10 per cent of the world's annual release of seismic energy.

Shortly before lunchtime on 1 September 1923 Japan was struck by its worst-ever earthquake, just as charcoal and gas braziers were cooking the midday meal in a million wooden houses. The capital, Tokyo, its international port Yokohama and the surrounding areas were subjected to between four and five minutes of shaking, followed shortly after by a tsunami – a seismic sea wave – 11 metres (35 feet) in height. Soon multiple

Ruins of the Grand Hotel, Yokohama, 1923, after the Great Kanto earthquake.

small fires started in panicked people's kitchens and, feeding on the congested houses, merged to form terrifying firestorms that burned through the night. By the morning of 3 September at least 140,000 people were dead and two-thirds of Tokyo, four-fifths of Yokohama, were ashes and debris. An area of Tokyo comprising 18 square kilometres (7 square miles) was incinerated (as compared with almost 13 square kilometres of San Francisco after its famous 1906 earthquake, and just 1.7 square kilometres of London in the Great Fire of 1666). Yokohama, with its preponderance of recent stone and brick structures built in imitation of a European city, suffered more from the shaking than fire-ravaged Tokyo. All that remained of Yokohama's Grand Hotel were piles of rubble. Even now, in the small sepia-toned photograph printed in the official report of 1926 of the Great Kanto earthquake introduced by Japan's prince regent, the future Emperor Hirohito, the utterly ruined Grand Hotel is an arresting sight. The photo's caption states baldly: 'No human work can withstand the violence of Nature.'[10]

After all great natural disasters the fearful survivors cannot help but look for someone to blame – whether it be mischievous animals and malicious devils, angry gods or incompetent governments and scientists, corrupt builders, foreign agents or sinful individuals.

In India, among the Hindus, the legend was of eight great elephants supporting the earth. When an elephant became weary from time to time, it lowered its head and gave it an earth-shattering shake. In Mongolia lamas imagined instead a gigantic frog carrying the earth on its back. The frog's periodic twitches produced earthquakes. Among the Tzotzil people of southern Mexico the story was of a cosmic jaguar scratching itself against the pillars of the world and causing earthquakes. The inhabitants of an island in Indonesia attributed earthquakes to a demon, which shook with rage when not propitiated by certain sacrifices.

In classical antiquity Poseidon, the Greek god of the sea, was usually considered to be responsible for earthquakes – perhaps not surprisingly, given the destructive power in the Aegean and Mediterranean of earthquake-induced tsunamis. Poseidon was said to cause earthquakes while striking his trident on the ground when he became annoyed. However, some Greek philosophers proposed natural, rather than divine, explanations for earthquakes. Thales, for example, writing around 580 BC, believed that the earth was floating on the oceans and that water movements were responsible for earthquakes. By contrast, Anaximenes, who also lived in the sixth century BC, proposed that rocks falling in the interior of the earth must strike other rocks and produce reverberations. Anaxagoras, during the fifth century BC, regarded fire as the cause of at least some earthquakes. Aristotle, a hundred or so years later, believed in a 'central fire' inside caverns in the earth from which flames, smoke and heat rapidly rose and burst violently through the surface rocks, causing both volcanic eruptions and earthquakes. As the subterranean fires burned away the rocks, the underground caverns would collapse, causing earthquakes. Aristotle even classified earthquakes into types according to whether they shook structures and people in mainly a vertical or a diagonal direction, and whether or not they were associated with escaping vapours. Much later, the Roman philosopher Seneca, inspired in part by an Italian earthquake in AD 62 or 63, proposed that the movement of air – rather than smoky vapours – trapped and compressed within the earth, was responsible for both violent storms and destructive rock movements.

Matthys Pool, 'Poseidon Sitting on a Shell', engraving, from Luigi Ferdinando Marsigli, *Histoire Physique de la Mer* (1725).

a *AMSTERDAM aux Depens de la* COMPAGNIE *1725.*

   In Catholic Europe the wrath of God was generally seen as the cause of earthquakes. Thus, after the shaking down and incineration of much of Lisbon in 1755, the Inquisition responded by charging some of the survivors with heresy and roasting them in the fires of the *auto-da-fé* – a response that helped to provoke the French rationalist Voltaire into writing his celebrated satire, *Candide*. In Spanish-ruled colonial South America sins against morality were invoked. Heinrich von Kleist's

1807 German novella, *Das Erdbeben in Chili* (*The Earthquake in Chile*) – based on a real earthquake in Santiago in 1647, according to its opening sentence, but apparently motivated by the great 1755 disaster at Lisbon – imagines the residents of a devastated Santiago blaming the earthquake on the behaviour of two adulterous lovers; the people proceed to club them to death. In North America the Yurok tribe interpreted the San Francisco earthquake of 1906 as punishment for white men who had stolen tribal artefacts and displayed them in museums in San Francisco and nearby Berkeley. Even in the mid-twentieth century Mahatma Gandhi could say, after a great earthquake in northern India in 1934: 'Visitations like droughts, floods, earthquakes and the like, though they seem to have only physical origins are, for me, somehow connected with men's morals.'[11]

In the Japanese tradition the most common explanation for earthquakes involved a *namazu*, a giant catfish living in the mud

Earthquake in a
16th-century drawing
by Jean Cousin
the Elder.

beneath the earth. The creature was normally restrained by a god who protected Japan from earthquakes by keeping a mighty rock on the *namazu*'s head. The supposed rock can be seen at Kashima, a place about 100 kilometres (60 miles) from Tokyo that has been comparatively free of earthquakes. However, the Kashima god would occasionally have to leave his post in order to confer with other gods. At such times the *namazu* was free to twitch its barbels, writhe around and generally play pranks – with disastrous results for human beings. The mythology is brilliantly and humorously depicted in coloured woodblock prints, known as *namazu-e*, made after an earthquake near Edo (modern Tokyo) in 1855. In one print, the restless catfish is seen being attacked by every inhabitant of Edo's red-light district except for the carpenters and other artisans, who inevitably do well out of earthquakes. Today images of catfish appear in emergency earthquake preparedness activities in Japan, such as the Earthquake Early Warning logo of the Japan Meteorological Agency.

By the time of the Great Kanto earthquake in 1923, however, the rapid spread of Western ideas and science in Japan meant that few Japanese believed in the tradition; indeed, *namazu-e* sold poorly in 1923, as compared with the outpouring of images in 1855. Instead of supernatural catfish, many residents of Tokyo pointed an accusing finger at Tokyo's immigrant Korean labouring community, a group generally despised by the native Japanese as a result of Japan's annexation of Korea in 1910. Following the fires a rumour swept through the darkened city that Korean saboteurs had started the conflagration and had also poisoned the wells; they were even said (by Japanese-owned newspapers) to be plotting the assassination of the Japanese imperial family. In the days that followed, between 6,000 and 10,000 Koreans were lynched by Japanese vigilantes, some of them with the connivance of nationalistic members of the military and police; the true number of massacred Koreans is unlikely to be established, in the absence of any official inquiry since 1923.

Japan's most famous film director, Akira Kurosawa – legendary for his dramatization of the extremes of human behaviour in such movies as *Rashomon*, *Seven Samurai* and *Throne of Blood* (a

version of *Macbeth*) – was a schoolboy of thirteen at the time of
the earthquake, living in a hilly suburb of Tokyo. His family
house was badly damaged and its electricity supply knocked
out along with the power in the rest of the city, but he and his
family were lucky to escape physically unscathed. In his fascinat-
ing and frank autobiography, written six decades later, Kurosawa
devotes three sections of the book – 'September 1, 1923', 'Darkness and humanity' and 'A horrifying excursion' – to the Great
Kanto earthquake. He observes: 'Through it I learnt not only of
the extraordinary powers of nature, but of extraordinary things
that lie in human hearts.'[12]

Kurosawa's military-minded father – something of a samurai
to his son – was mistaken for a foreigner while going in search
of missing relatives in a burned-out area because of his full
beard. He was surrounded by a mob wielding clubs, who dis-
persed only when he thundered 'Idiots!' at them in Japanese. At
home the young Akira was told to keep watch at night with a
wooden sword in his hand over a drainage pipe, narrow enough

Namazu (catfish)
attacked by inhabitants
of Edo (Tokyo)
following the Ansei
earthquake, 1855,
woodblock print.

for a crawling cat, in case Koreans were able to sneak through it. He was warned, too, not to drink the water from a neighbourhood well because its surrounding wall carried white chalk marks written in a strange Korean code. But the grimly absurd truth was that Akira himself had been responsible for these meaningless scribbles.

When the holocaust in central Tokyo had died down, Kurosawa recalls how his elder brother invited him to take a look at the ruins:

I set out to accompany my brother with the kind of cheerfulness you feel on a school excursion. By the time I realized how horrifying this excursion would be and tried to shrink back from it, it was already too late. My brother ignored my hesitation and dragged me along . . .

At first we saw only an occasional burned body, but as we drew closer to the downtown area, the numbers increased. But my brother took me by the hand and walked on with determination. The burned landscape for as far as the eye· could see had a brownish red colour . . . Amid this expanse of nauseating redness lay every kind of corpse imaginable. I saw corpses charred black, half-burned corpses, corpses in gutters, corpses floating in rivers, corpses piled up on bridges, corpses blocking off a whole street at an intersection, and every manner of death possible to human beings displayed by corpses. When I involuntarily looked away, my brother scolded me, 'Akira, look carefully now.'

. . . In some places the piles of corpses formed little mountains. On top of one of these mountains sat a blackened body in the lotus position of Zen meditation. This corpse looked exactly like a Buddhist statue. My brother and I stared at it for a long time, standing stock still. Then my brother, as if talking to himself, softly said, 'Magnificent, isn't it?' I felt the same way . . .

The night we returned from the horrifying excursion I was fully prepared to be unable to sleep, or to have terrible nightmares if I did. But no sooner had I laid my head on the pillow than it was morning. I had slept like a log, and I couldn't remember anything frightening from my dreams. This seemed so strange to me that I asked my brother how it could have come about. 'If you shut your eyes to a frightening sight, you end up being frightened. If you look at everything straight on, there is nothing to be afraid of.' Looking back on the excursion now, I realize that it must have been horrifying for my brother too. It had been an expedition to conquer fear.[13]

Tokyo was rebuilt within about seven years, essentially where it had been before. Today, vastly expanded and more prosperous, Tokyo is considered by the Japanese government to be at high risk of suffering another destructive earthquake, given that it was struck in 1855 and 1923 but has escaped severe damage since then. In 1995 a totally unanticipated earthquake 500 kilometres (310 miles) to the west of the capital, which destroyed parts of the port of Kobe and killed more than 6,400 people, provided some idea of the likely future chaos in metropolitan Tokyo — not to speak of the psychological cost to the Japanese, as suggested by the short stories in novelist Haruki Murakami's collection *after the quake*. Murakami's first story opens with a married woman in Tokyo glued to a television set for five whole days, 'staring at crumbled banks and hospitals, whole blocks of stores in flames, severed rail lines and expressways' in quake-struck Kobe. This nihilistic media exposure drives the woman to divorce her husband, abandoning him with just a note on the kitchen table saying that 'living with you is like living with a chunk of air'.[14] When her former husband later tries to have sex with a woman, he gives up, because he cannot forget the silent images of 'highways, flames, smoke, piles of rubble, cracks in streets' running through his mind like a slideshow.[15]

Around the world, more than 60 large cities — in every continent except Australia — are at risk from earthquakes on the basis of their seismic history. They include such conurbations as Beijing, Cairo, Calcutta, Delhi, Istanbul, Jakarta, Lima, Los Angeles, Mexico City, the San Francisco Bay Area, Seoul,

Shanghai, Singapore, Tehran and, of course, Tokyo and Yokohama. Although European cities as a whole have been comparatively less affected, highly destructive earthquakes have struck Athens, Bucharest, Lisbon, Madrid, Messina, Milan, Naples, Rome, Turin and many other Italian towns and cities during the past three centuries.

In the central Italian city of L'Aquila, for example, a relatively small – magnitude-6.3 – earthquake killed 309 people and caused much destruction in 2009. L'Aquila had been largely destroyed by earthquakes before, in 1461 and 1703. The disaster of 2009 would quickly have been forgotten outside Italy were it not for its bizarre aftershock. For the first time in the world the authorities of a city struck by an earthquake brought a charge of manslaughter against scientific experts on earthquake hazards. L'Aquila's public prosecutor accused six government scientists

Earthquake destruction, L'Aquila, Italy, 2009.

and one government official of underestimating the seismic risk, thereby encouraging residents to stay in their homes and expose themselves to unnecessary danger. The international seismological community was shocked and outraged. Although seismologists can predict where to expect most earthquakes, with the help of plate tectonic theory, they know that they are still far from being able to predict the precise locations and timings of major shocks, despite periodic claims to the contrary.

Earthquake disasters have at least one benefit: they educate seismologists. The naturalist Charles Darwin, who was also a significant geologist, wrote in his classic travel journal *The Voyage of the Beagle* that his experience of an earthquake in the city of Concepción on the coast of Chile was perhaps the single most interesting event of his entire five-year expedition around the world between 1831 and 1836. Just after the earthquake occurred in February 1835, an excited Darwin recorded:

> It is a bitter and humiliating thing to see works, which
> have cost men so much time and labour, overthrown in
> one minute; yet compassion for the inhabitants is almost
> instantly forgotten, from the interest excited in finding that
> state of things produced in a moment of time, which one
> is accustomed to attribute to the succession of ages.[16]

Yet, for all the amazing advances in seismological science and earthquake-resistant engineering during the second half of the twentieth century, and the improved disaster preparedness of governments and international aid agencies, earthquakes continue to cause immense loss of life, property damage and infrastructural damage in the early twenty-first century. The Indian Ocean earthquake of 2004 (also known as the Sumatra-Andaman earthquake), with a magnitude of 9.1–9.3, created a tsunami that killed more than 230,000 people in fourteen countries, the worst affected being Indonesia, Sri Lanka, India and Thailand. In 2010 the magnitude-7.0 earthquake that struck Haiti very close to the capital, Port-au-Prince, wrecked much of the city and took many tens of thousands of lives, according to reliable estimates made in 2011 (more than 300,000 lives, according to the Haitian government). A pair of earthquakes near Christchurch, in New Zealand, six months apart in 2010 and 2011, took far fewer lives (181 fatalities) than the Indian Ocean and Haiti quakes, as is typical of earthquakes in developed countries. But instead they cost the government, insurance companies, businesses and individual householders many billions in US dollars. The second New Zealand earthquake, though only of magnitude 6.3, caused such widespread weakening of the soil beneath Christchurch through the shaking process known as liquefaction that parts of the city – including more than 5,000 homes – were declared uneconomical to rebuild. The damage made this comparatively small earthquake New Zealand's most costly natural disaster by far, and the third costliest earthquake disaster ever, after the magnitude-6.7 Northridge earthquake near

Earthquake damage, Jacmel, Haiti, 2010.

Los Angeles in 1994 and the magnitude-9.0 Tohoku-Oki earthquake in 2011.

No one will ever forget the crisis provoked by the second of these latter two disasters (also known as the Great East Japan earthquake), which was described by the then Japanese prime minister as the 'toughest and most difficult crisis for the country' since the Second World War.[17] The epicentre was under the Pacific Ocean, 70 kilometres (43 miles) off the east coast of Japan near the Japan Trench, and the predictable result was yet another Japanese tsunami, which in this instance reached a staggering maximum height of 39 metres (128 feet). The waves not only drowned well over 20,000 people but overwhelmed the Fukushima Daiichi nuclear power plant. The damage to its operating systems precipitated a core meltdown, the most serious nuclear accident since the Chernobyl disaster in 1986, and a rethinking

Earthquake damage, Christchurch, New Zealand, 2010.

Tsunami destruction of Miyako, Japan, following the Tohoku-Oki earthquake, 2011.

of the dangers of nuclear power both in Japan and worldwide. This led the German government to announce that it would close its nuclear power stations by 2022.

The power of earthquakes, coupled with the fires that follow them, is certainly awesome. Pompeii was so damaged by an earthquake in AD 62 or 63 that the Roman emperor Nero, after a visit, recommended the city be abandoned. Antioch, a trading and pleasure city on the shores of Asia Minor, was devastated four times by earthquakes in AD 115, 458, 526 and 528. In central America Antigua, the capital of Guatemala, was ruined four times from 1586 in less than 300 years; Managua, the capital of Nicaragua, ten times in fewer than two centuries. Yet all these cities – as well as ruined Lisbon, San Francisco and Tokyo, of course – were rebuilt on the same site as before, and flourished, with the exception of Pompeii, which had the misfortune to be buried by the volcanic eruption of Vesuvius in AD 79. The only major city in the historical record to have been more or less abandoned after an earthquake and tsunami is Port Royal in Jamaica, much of which literally slid under the sea in 1692.

How influential in history have earthquakes really been, for all their horrors? Certainly less influential than Darwin imagined in Chile in 1835 after examining the ruins of Concepción, when he darkly contemplated what would happen to England

Relief from a house
in Pompeii depicting
destruction by the
earthquake of AD 62
or 63.

in the event of a major earthquake, and noted in his journal:
'Earthquakes alone are sufficient to destroy the prosperity of
any country.'[18] That said, a fairly convincing case can be made
for a long-term decline in Portugal's power and influence as a consequence of the destruction of its capital, Lisbon, in 1755. Undoubtedly, if we accept the account given by Latin America's
liberator, Simón Bolívar, it was an earthquake in Venezuela in 1812
that directly influenced Bolívar's freeing of Bolivia, Colombia,
Ecuador, Peru and Venezuela from Spanish colonial rule in the

Ruins of the
cathedral at Concepción,
Chile, following the
earthquake of 1835,
engraving.

Earthquake destruction, Port Royal, Jamaica, 1692, engraving.

1820s. For this earthquake precipitated the collapse of Bolívar's first republican government of Venezuela under Spanish attack, forcing him into exile, where he became the leader of a much wider independence movement than the one he had led in Venezuela. In Japan the massive cost of rebuilding Tokyo in the 1920s, closely followed by the worldwide economic depression of the 1930s, produced an economic stress that led to the militarization of Japanese society and eventually to Japan's entry into the Second World War. In Mexico the ruling party's failure to deal with the aftermath of the Mexico City earthquake in 1985

Ruins of City Hall, San
Francisco, following the
earthquake and fire of
1906.

distinctly weakened the sclerotic hold on power it had had since
the 1920s. And in Sri Lanka the Indian Ocean earthquake of
2004 helped to solidify the grip of a strongly nationalist government dominated by the majority Sinhalese, which soon took the
decision to annihilate the minority separatist movement led by
the Tamil Tigers.

At a much earlier period in history, it is possible, though
unproven, that earthquakes played a greater role in the decline of
cities and civilizations. It is difficult to be sure from the available
record. The first reliable reports of earthquakes begin only in
780 BC in China, in 464 BC in Greece and in AD 416 in Japan,
although there is a report in the ancient Chinese *Bamboo Annals*
of the shaking of Taishan mountain in Shandong province
dated as early as 1831 BC. Very likely it was an earthquake that
destroyed the biblical cities of Sodom and Gomorrah, judging
from the description of their fate in the book of Genesis; there
is no certainty, since the cities' archaeological sites have yet to
be discovered. Earthquakes are also strong candidates to explain
other events of the Bible, such as the collapse of the walls of
Jericho and the parting of the Red Sea. They may have been a
factor in the catastrophic end of the Bronze Age civilizations in

overleaf:
Jan Brueghel the Elder,
Sodom and Gomorrah,
17th century, painting.

29

Turkey, Greece and Crete during a period of around 50 years in the late second millennium BC: that is, the fall of Troy, Mycenae, Knossos and other cities, which left behind substantial archaeological sites. There is also tantalizing evidence for a seismic role in the fall of Armageddon (Megiddo) in Israel, Petra in Jordan and Teotihuacan in Mexico.

However, archaeologists are divided on the importance of earthquakes in the development of civilization. Most present-day archaeologists claim that earthquakes have had little to do with historical demises. They prefer to attribute the collapse of civilizations to human agency: war, invasion, social oppression, environmental abuse and so on. The conventional explanation of the Bronze Age collapse involves maritime invasion by the mysterious Sea Peoples, whose identities have long eluded scholars. 'When a city is destroyed for no apparent reason, archaeologists are far more comfortable ascribing the destruction to the vagaries of an unknown enemy than to the whims of nature', writes the geophysicist Amos Nur in *Apocalypse: Earthquakes, Archaeology, and the Wrath of God*.[19] There were notable exceptions: some

Throne Room, palace of Knossos, Crete, as recreated by the archaeologist Arthur Evans.

'Decapitated' victim of an earthquake in Jericho, *c.* 1400 BC. In fact the skeleton was decapitated not by the earthquake but by subsequent fault movement, indicated by the crack.

academics during the first half of the twentieth century were sympathetic to the idea that earthquakes could crush civilizations. They included Arthur Evans, the first excavator of Knossos, Carl Blegen, who excavated Troy, and Claude Schaeffer, the author of a controversial book on the subject published in 1948. But the majority of academics have always been sceptical. For instance, Robert Drews took pains to quash any earthquake explanation in *The End of the Bronze Age: Changes in Warfare and the Catastrophe ca. 1200 BC*, and Jared Diamond made no mention of earthquakes or volcanic eruptions in *Collapse: How Societies Choose to Fail or Succeed*. If earthquakes really have had so great an influence, the sceptics ask, then where is the hard evidence?

This is what Nur attempts to provide in *Apocalypse*. Drawing upon the evidence from archaeological sites, especially in his native Israel, Nur demonstrates how earthquakes may be detected in the archaeological record by analysing geological formations, faults, structural movement, human remains, the collapse of pillars and walls, and inscriptions. In Jericho, for example, he notes that its excavators found grain under the fallen walls of the city, along with the skeletons of two people killed by the walls' collapse. Had the city simply been conquered by an enemy, without the prior collapse of its walls due to an earthquake, the valuable grain would surely have been seized by the invaders. In

33

Part of the Apocalypse cycle painted on the walls of the medieval Church of the Virgin Mary, Karlštejn Castle, Czech Republic, depicting an earthquake.

Mycenae, he notes that the immense stone blocks of the city's outer wall are built on top of a fault scarp, which must have been created by a major earthquake. By superimposing upon a map of the Bronze Age sites in the eastern Mediterranean that were destroyed between 1225 and 1175 BC a second map of the maximum intensity of seismic ground motion between AD 1900 and 1980, which overlaps remarkably with the first map, Nur postulates that strong seismic ground motion in ancient times, too, may have helped to destroy these Bronze Age cultures. While none of his evidence is conclusive, it is more than merely suggestive. In the ancient world, as in the modern, such earth-shattering events of nature were surely – at least sometimes – influential in changing the course of human history.

2 Lisbon, 1755: The Wrath of God

The ruination of Lisbon by an earthquake in the middle of the eighteenth century had an influence on contemporary European life and thought comparable with the psychic shock waves produced by the destruction of Hiroshima by an atomic bomb in the mid-twentieth century. In the century that followed, the Lisbon earthquake became as iconic an image of natural disaster as the volcanic eruption of Vesuvius in AD 79 that buried the ancient Roman city of Pompeii – the ruins of which were rediscovered in 1749, by chance at about the same time as the earthquake occurred.

Thus in 1848 – the year of revolutions in Europe – the newly refurbished Colosseum in London's Regent's Park staged a hugely successful exhibition telling the story of Lisbon's earthquake, tsunami and fire on 1 November 1755 through the medium of 'moveable paintings' accompanied by dramatic music. The *Illustrated London News* described in rapt detail the experience of seeing this 'Cyclorama of Lisbon'. In the opening scenes, said the magazine,

> We are presented with the beautiful, varied, and sublime scenery of the [River] Tagus, the movement of which produces a peculiar feeling in the spectator. The theatre in which he sits seems like a vessel floating down the stream, and passing one object after another – the mountainous shore – the ships and vessels, the merchantmen and the *xebec* [Mediterranean trading ships] – the nunnery, the fort, the mansion, the palace,

the various convents, the Consulate House, and, at length, the City, with its palatial, ecclesiastical, public and private buildings – all doomed to sudden destruction. The last scene presents the Grand Square of Lisbon, 'with its gorgeous palaces and magnificent ranges of streets, massive arches and noble flights of steps, vases, and other colossal decorations, with the beautiful statue and fountain of Apollo.'[1]

The soundtrack consisted of excerpts from classical works such as Beethoven's 'Pastoral' Symphony, Mozart's *Don Giovanni*, Mendelssohn's 'Wedding March' and Haydn's 'Il Terremoto' ('The Earthquake'), plus a Portuguese dance and a Brazilian melody – since it was Brazilian gold mined in Portugal's South American colony that had provided the funds to build up Lisbon in this period. The music was blasted out by a grand organ with sixteen pedals and 2,407 pipes, an Apollonicon built by Bevington & Sons of Soho, played by a Mr Pittman. When the earthquake struck there was the sound of a 'subterranean roar', followed by an 'appalling crash' during which the stage was plunged into darkness.

Then the magazine reported the awful scene after the lights came up again:

Destruction of Lisbon depicted in a German etching, 1756.

We next see the ships tossing upon the waves, fated to the destruction with which the lowering sky only too visibly threatens them. All is terror and despair. But this passes, and the site of the city returns, now covered with ruins where so lately we contemplated the glories of architectural genius – all, by the visitation of an inscrutable Providence, involved in one common wreck, with more than 30,000 of its dwellers.

Overall, said the *Illustrated London News*, 'A more magnificent series of pictorial wonders cannot be imagined.' So widely appreciated was this Colosseum 'cyclorama' that it continued into the 1850s. In 1851 it successfully competed against a display about the destruction of Pompeii at the Great Exhibition.

A few years later, in 1858, the writer Charles Dickens felt the allure of the century-old Lisbon disaster while on a visit to Portugal. In his journal, *Household Words*, Dickens conjured up the dreadful contrast brought about by the earthquake:

That night, looking from the Braganca [Hotel] window at the weltering bay which seemed turned to silver, over which highway I could see away to Belem, the guarded mouth of the Tagus, I beheld the tranquil terraced roofs below, quiet in the moonlight; for the wilful Mohammedan moon was in her crescent, and I could almost imagine myself in the old Moorish city. As I looked, I fell into a reverie in my chair in the Bragança balcony. Napier's *Peninsular War* dropping from my hand, I imagined myself, that November morning, on that safe roof-top watching that tranquil city. Suddenly, the houses all around me began to roll and tremble like a stormy sea. Through an eclipse dimness I saw the buildings round my feet and far away on every side, gape and split; the floors fell with the shake of cannons. The groans and cries of a great battle were round me. I could hear the sea dashing on the quays, and rising to swallow what the earthquake had left. Through the air, dark with falling walls and beams, amid showers of stones red with

the billows of fire from sudden conflagrations, I saw the
cloudy streets strewn with the dead and dying; screaming
crowds, running thickly, hither and thither, like sheep when
the doors of the red slaughter-house are closed.[2]

Today, however, the destruction of Lisbon is largely forgotten
– unlike the destruction of Pompeii. '9 out of 10 well-educated,
well-travelled Europeans are still unaware of it', admits Edward
Paice in *Wrath of God*, his engaging account of the earthquake.[3]
Even some academic specialists in the period neglect the disaster.
'It is a source of great puzzlement', comments leading geogra-
pher Peter Gould, 'that this devastating environmental event,
right at the centre of the century of the Enlightenment, so often
leaves hardly a trace in many standard works by biographers and
historians.' If Voltaire had not written his celebrated poem on
the disaster in 1755, followed by his story *Candide* in 1759, 'one
wonders whether the event might have disappeared from human
memory altogether', writes Gould.[4]

Perhaps this surprising amnesia can be explained, at least to
some extent. Archaeologists, as we already know, neglect earthquakes and other natural disasters as explanations of cultural
change, preferring to look for human agency. On the whole, so
do historians. That is why Hiroshima and Auschwitz will most
likely never be forgotten as universal symbols of twentieth-
century disaster, whereas San Francisco and Tokyo have much
less global resonance, despite their earthquake-related catastro-
phes. Pompeii – almost uniquely among natural disasters – is
still remembered the world over, partly because its residents
intensified their predicament by refusing to heed the warnings
from Vesuvius of its imminent eruption. The Lisbon earthquake,
by contrast, struck without any foreshocks, giving no one in the
city the slightest chance to escape its consequences.

Moreover, the ruins of Pompeii, of course, exist and have
attracted millions of spectators, whereas the ruins of Lisbon –
much visited in their day by tourists with a fascination for Gothic
melancholy – were eventually cleared away to rebuild a new city.
In addition, Portuguese writers avoided the earthquake as a

subject for memoirs and secular literature, not only at the time but also in the decades thereafter. There is no Portuguese equivalent of Voltaire's poem about the earthquake. No memorable contemporary record of the earthquake's effect on Portuguese life was written, unlike, for example, the responses of Japanese writers in the period after the Great Kanto earthquake in Tokyo and the much later reflections penned by Akira Kurosawa in his autobiography. Indeed, almost everything we know about what actually happened in Lisbon on All Saints' Day in November 1755 and on the days that followed comes from the horrified accounts of affected foreigners, many of them resident British merchants pursuing a lucrative trade with Portugal. Portuguese witnesses of the earthquake, traumatized by events and operating under the watchful eyes of the court and government, the clergy and the Inquisition, were reluctant to express themselves on paper.

In general, it is fair to say that if Portugal had been a more influential country in 1755, then the Lisbon earthquake might well be better remembered today. But in truth, despite Lisbon's financial wealth and considerable size – it was probably Europe's fourth largest city after London, Paris and Naples – Portugal was regarded throughout Europe as an economic, political and intellectual backwater. It manufactured almost nothing and imported almost everything, including its textiles, toys, watches, chandlery, arms and shot from England, which were paid for with gold from Minas Gerais in Brazil – to the tune of more than £25 million sent to London by the middle of the century. Its ruler for the first half of the century, João v, spent his one-fifth share of these massive Brazilian revenues (the rate of the royal tax on the gold trade) on the construction of monuments and palaces. He was reputed to be the richest monarch in Europe, and therefore rarely needed to assemble his court. When he became ill in 1742 affairs of state fell into the hands of the clergy: cardinals and priests, notably the Jesuit confessor of the king. By 1750 Portugal had perhaps 200,000 clergy in a population of fewer than three million people, and was 'more priest ridden than any other country in the world, with the possible exception of Tibet', according to the distinguished historian of Portugal and the Far East C. R. Boxer.[5] In that year João v died, on the very same day as a slight earthquake in Lisbon. His son and successor, José i, was chiefly interested in riding, playing cards, attending the theatre and opera, and worshipping God.

Although there were no tremors heralding the earthquake of 1755, it was preceded by some ominous natural phenomena in Lisbon and other parts of the country. The weather was different from usual, as often seems to be the case before great earthquakes. The day before it struck, 31 October, was warm for the season, noted the consul of Hamburg, who was surprised to see a fog rolling in from the sea, since this was normally a phenomenon seen in the summer. Then the wind blew the fog back to sea, where it became as thick as the consul could ever recall seeing it. Behind the receding fog, he thought he could hear the sea 'rise with a prodigious roaring'.[6] All along the coast, the evening tide was late by two hours, causing wary fishermen to haul their boats further up the beach. Around the same time a village fountain was observed to run almost dry. Elsewhere, a well dried up altogether. A physician noted that for several days there had been complaints about an odd taste in Lisbon's water supply. In another place the air had a sulphurous smell. Animals, too, behaved abnormally, which is again a common observation before great earthquakes. Dogs, mules and caged birds became unaccountably agitated. Rabbits and other animals left their burrows. Worms crawled to the surface in large numbers.

But no one had sufficient experience to anticipate an earthquake. Lisbon had been struck hard once before, in 1531, when about 30,000 people had died. It had been severely shaken, too, though much less damagingly, in 1724, within living memory. And in 1750 it had received another shaking (on the day of the king's death). However, this latest earthquake had been too slight to disturb anyone's complacency – unlike that of people in London the same year.

The violent shaking of 1755 began around 9.30 a.m. on 1 November. It lasted for about ten minutes, as compared with four to five minutes for the 1923 Great Kanto earthquake in Tokyo,

View of Lisbon
from the River Tagus
before the earthquake,
engraving.

eight seconds for the 1994 earthquake in Northridge, California, and about five seconds for the Great English earthquake of 1884 in Colchester. It came in three distinct waves separated by a pause of no more than a minute, of which the second wave was the greatest, with a magnitude later estimated by seismologists to be 8.5–8.8 on the evidence of the level of destruction. Within a mere quarter of an hour the great city was 'laid in ruins', noted the British consul.[7] Tremors continued all through the day and night with no more than a quarter of an hour's respite, culminating in the biggest aftershock since the first day a week later, on 8 November. In 1761 there was a further major earthquake. It shook the city for at least three minutes and possibly as long as five, during which many of the ruins of 1755 finally collapsed.

Since 1 November was All Saints' Day, many Lisboetas were attending Mass in the city's numerous and lavish churches when the shaking began. The coincidence was a horrible one for the worshippers, who were crushed under a rain of falling masonry as many churches quickly crumbled. The palace of the Inquisition fell, too, as did the magnificent new opera house – its scheduled evening performance of *A Destruição de Troya* (*The Destruction*

of Troy) forever cancelled. Other people were incinerated in the conflagration started by kitchen fires (as in Tokyo in 1923). The blaze was so intense that the ruins were still too hot, seventeen days after the disaster, for merchants and others facing financial ruin to search for their valuables. Yet others were drowned by a tsunami. Every Lisboeta who saw the wall of water rushing in from the River Tagus knew what it was, because they had all heard of the swamping of the Peruvian port of Callao and the deaths of up to 10,000 people after a great earthquake in Lima in 1746. The Lisbon sea wave reached a height of 12 metres (40 feet) and flooded the streets, squares and gardens up to 180 metres from the waterfront; it returned twice thereafter. The waves swept away the splendid new quay that ran along the river in front of the Customs House, along with hundreds of desperate people who had been waiting on the quayside for boats. At the mouth of the Tagus it hurled boulders weighing as much as 25 tons some 27 metres inland. On the south coast of Portugal, the Algarve, the seabed was exposed in places to a depth of 37 metres, and the first sea wave was up to 30 metres in height.

Jacques-Philippe Le Bas, ruins of St Nicholas Church, Lisbon, 1757, etching.

The devastation there, except at Faro (which was protected by a lagoon), was so extensive that it was still unrepaired in the early twentieth century.

A British surgeon in Lisbon, Richard Wolfall, who attended the wounded from noon until night on that first day, did his best to evoke the doom-laden atmosphere of the catastrophe in a letter written to a friend some weeks later:

> The shocking sight of the dead bodies, together with the shrieks and cries of those, who were half-buried in the ruins, are only known to those who were eye-witnesses. It far exceeds all description, for the fear and consternation were so great, that the most resolute person durst not stay a moment to remove a few stones off the friend he loved most, though many might have been saved by so doing: but nothing was thought of but self-preservation; getting into open spaces, and into the middle of streets, was the most probable security. Such as were in the upper storeys of houses, were in general more fortunate than those, that attempted to escape by the doors; for they were buried under the ruins with the greatest part of the foot-passengers: such as were in equipages escaped best, though their cattle and drivers suffered severely; but those lost in houses and the streets were very unequal in number to those, that were buried in the ruins of churches ... all the churches in the city were vastly crouded, and the number of churches here exceeds that of both London and Westminster.
>
> Had the misery ended there, it might in some degree admitted of redress; for though lives could not be restored, yet the immense riches, that were in the ruins, might in some part have been digged out: but the hopes of this are almost gone, for in about two hours after the shock, fires broke out in three different parts of the city, occasioned from the goods and the kitchen-fires being all jumbled together ... Indeed every element seemed to conspire to our destruction; for soon after the shock, which was near

high water the tide rose 40 feet higher in an instant than was ever known, and as suddenly subsided. Had it not so done, the whole city must have been laid under water. As soon as we had time for recollection, nothing but death was present in our imaginations.[8]

The total number of fatalities from the earthquake, fire and tsunami is uncertain. The best estimate is 30,000–40,000 deaths in Lisbon and a further 10,000 in the rest of Portugal, Morocco and Spain. (Recall that 'more than 30,000' deaths in Lisbon were mentioned by the *Illustrated London News* a century after the earthquake.) All the hospitals in the city had been shaken or burned to the ground, along with the prisons and the record offices of the municipal authorities. Three-quarters of the city's principal religious institutions had gone or were severely damaged; there was no parish church remaining in at least 30 of the 40 parishes. As for the financial cost of the damage, it was of the order of 20 times the value of the cargoes in that autumn's fleets

Leonardo Rodriguez helps to free his daughter from the rubble of the Lisbon earthquake, watched over by the Holy Mother and Child, painting. The inscription records that Rodriguez commissioned the painting in gratitude for the miraculous survival of his child.

from Brazil, or three times the losses sustained by London in the Great Fire of 1666.

The exact epicentre of the earthquake is also uncertain. Undoubtedly it lay in the Atlantic Ocean, hence the production of the tsunami. It was probably some 200 kilometres (125 miles) west-southwest of Cape Saint Vincent, judging partly by a magnitude-7.3 earthquake in this area in 1969 with a similar (though less intense) spatial pattern of seismicity, which also generated a tsunami. This would put the epicentre in the Azores-Gibraltar fault zone, near a fault line running from the Azores through the Strait of Gibraltar into the Mediterranean – at the junction of the African and Eurasian tectonic plates.

On the Atlantic island of Madeira, a Portuguese colony further to the southwest of Cape Saint Vincent on the other side

Part of a mass grave containing more than 3,000 earthquake victims, discovered beneath the Academy of Sciences, Lisbon, 2004.

45

of the epicentre, the inhabitants heard a rumbling noise in the air 'like that of empty carriages passing hastily over a stone pavement', and then their houses shook at 9.38 a.m. for about a minute, according to a resident shipper of Madeira wine.[9] But there were no casualties and hardly any damage. At the Rock of Gibraltar itself, on the south coast of Spain, some of the guns of the British battery were seen to rise, others to fall, as a result of the seismic undulations. Elsewhere in Europe and North Africa the shaking was sensible at a distance of 2,400 kilometres (1,500 miles). Its effects were felt over an astonishing area of almost 16 million square kilometres (6 million square miles); that is, twice the size of Australia. The earthquake produced seiches (fluctuations in water levels) in the lakes of Britain, including an extraordinary agitation of Loch Ness in Scotland with a substantial wave that threatened a brewery near the loch's waterline. In Finland, 3,500 kilometres from the probable epicentre, it disturbed the water at the port of Turku (Åbo). The tsunami proved to be even more far-reaching. It brought pandemonium to parts of the coasts of Cornwall, the southwestern peninsula of England. On the far side of the Atlantic, at the islands of the Caribbean, the sea retreated as much as a mile, beaching a ship that had been floating in 4.5 metres (15 feet) of water in the Netherlands Antilles, and then rose 6.5 metres, flooding low land and the upper rooms of houses in the French West Indies.

For the first time ever following a great earthquake, data were systematically collected. Under the direction of a reforming prime minister who forcefully took charge of the government's response to the disaster – Sebastião José de Carvalho e Melo (best known under his later title, as the first marquess of Pombal) – an official questionnaire was distributed to parishes. Its thirteen questions covered matters such as the timing and direction of the earthquake; the numbers of aftershocks and previous earthquakes; the earthquake's effects on bodies of water, including fountains and wells; the size of any fissures; the movements of the sea before the tsunami; the number of deaths; the duration of fires; the damage to buildings; food shortages; and the immediate measures taken by those in authority, whether civil, military or ecclesiastical. For instance: did you perceive the shock to be greater from one direction than another? Did buildings seem to fall more to one side than the other? Did the sea rise or fall first? How many hands did it rise above the normal? The answers were stored in the national historical archives in Lisbon, where they can still be read. As the historian of earthquakes Charles Davison remarked, the Lisbon earthquake was the first earthquake 'to be investigated on modern scientific lines'.[10]

In Britain data on the effects of the Lisbon earthquake were collected from all over the country and abroad by the Royal Society, supplementing the data collected after the British earthquakes in 1750. John Michell, an astronomer at Cambridge University, took up the challenge of analysing the eyewitness reports and accounting for earthquake motions in terms of Newtonian mechanics. Michell eventually produced an important, if flawed, geological paper, 'Conjectures Concerning the Cause and Observations upon the Phaenomena of Earthquakes', which was published in the Royal Society's *Philosophical Transactions* for 1760.

Michell correctly concluded that earthquakes were 'waves set up by shifting masses of rock miles below the surface', although his explanation for this shifting relied wrongly on explosions of steam as underground water encountered underground fires.[11] When the shifting occurred beneath the seabed, he also rightly concluded that it would produce a sea wave as well as an earthquake. There were two types of earthquake wave, he said, once again coming close to the truth: the first was a 'tremulous' vibration within the earth, followed shortly by an undulation of the earth's surface. From this he argued that the speed of an earthquake wave could be determined by its arrival times at different points on the surface. Such times were known approximately from eyewitness reports on far-flung places affected by the Lisbon earthquake, which enabled Michell to calculate a speed for its wave of 1,930 kilometres (1,200 miles) per hour. He was the first scientist to attempt such a calculation – inaccurate though it was, and unaware though he was that the speed of seismic waves varies with the types of rock through which they pass. He then went further by theorizing that the surface origin of an earthquake, what we now call its epicentre, could be located by combining the arrival-time data. Although he curiously chose a different – and inaccurate – way to calculate the epicentre of the Lisbon earthquake, relying instead on reports of the direction of the tsunami, Michell's theoretical principle for locating an epicentre is the basis of the method used today.

Despite being a clergyman, Michell left God out of his analysis – a sign of the Enlightenment times in which he was writing. But another scientifically minded English clergyman, William Warburton, later bishop of Gloucester, found himself struggling to come to terms with the Lisbon disaster without invoking God. 'To suppose these desolations the scourge of heaven for human impieties, is a dreadful reflection', Warburton confided to a friend, 'and yet to suppose ourselves in a forlorn and fatherless world, is ten times a more frightful consideration.'[12] The Catholic clergy in Lisbon were put in an especially awkward position by the earthquake. If it really was divine punishment for the sins of Lisboetas, then why had it destroyed so many religious institutions and killed so many clergy? Although official accounts mention only a few hundred deaths of clerics, friars and nuns, the real figure was unquestionably far greater given their preponderance in Lisbon at the time; the true number must have been suppressed by the church authorities.

Voltaire, after the earthquake, was incensed by both the religiosity of the Catholic Church and the optimistic outlook of secular society. Optimism as a philosophy sprang from the influential ideas of the philosopher and mathematician Gottfried Leibniz and the poet and essayist Alexander Pope. Leibniz had conceived the world to be 'the best of all possible worlds' in a famous essay on good and evil published in 1710. Pope, in a celebrated poem of 1734–5, *An Essay on Man*, had declared:

> All Nature is but Art, unknown to thee;
> All Chance, Direction, which thou canst not see;
> All Discord, Harmony not understood;
> All partial Evil, universal Good.

And, spite of Pride, in erring Reason's spite,
One truth is clear, Whatever is, is right.[13]

A few days after hearing the first news of the Lisbon disaster, on 24 November, Voltaire informed a banker friend in Lyons:

> What a sad game of chance the game of human life is! What will the preachers say, especially if the palace of the Inquisition remains standing? I flatter myself at least that the reverend Fathers, the Inquisitors, will have been crushed like all the others. That ought to teach men not to persecute men, for while some holy scoundrels burn a few fanatics the earth swallows up the lot of them whole.[14]

In his poem about the earthquake, published anonymously in Paris in January 1756, Voltaire asked how either the church authorities, or the optimists, could possibly justify the destruction of Lisbon. Why not decadent London or Paris? Why does Lisbon lie in ruins, while in Paris they dance? he wrote. Later, in the Lisbon earthquake section of *Candide*, he satirized three typical reactions to the tragedy – that of the common man, the philosopher (Dr Pangloss) and the innocent (Candide):

> The sailor said with a whistle and an oath: 'There'll be some rich pickings here.'
> 'What can be the sufficient reason for this phenomenon?' wondered Pangloss.
> 'The end of the world is come!' Candide shouted.[15]

Portugal's prime minister, Pombal, came close to agreeing with Voltaire's attitude. Immediately after the earthquake the practical prime minister is famously supposed to have advised the pious king: 'What now? We bury the dead and heal the living.' Decrees were immediately issued to forbid the clergy from stirring up feelings of recrimination and guilt in the population. When the leader of the Jesuits, Gabriel Malagrida, prophesied a second great earthquake in November 1756, Pombal banished him. Three years later Pombal had the entire Jesuit order expelled from Portuguese territory. In 1761 Malagrida was subjected to an *auto-da-fé* in Lisbon by the Inquisition (now led by Pombal's brother) and garrotted; his corpse was then burned at the stake, and his ashes thrown into the Tagus. Meanwhile, the increasingly dictatorial Pombal pursued the rebuilding of the city. This continued well beyond his own fall from power in 1777 after the death of his royal patron, José I, and the occurrence of two further earthquakes in 1796 and 1801, into the nineteenth century.

Over the decades Lisbon recovered most of its former prosperity. But it continued to be haunted by a sense of deep loss,

Open-air Mass on the 250th anniversary of the Lisbon earthquake, held in the ruins of the Convento do Carmo, Lisbon, 2005.

Louis-Michel van Loo,
Marquess of Pombal,
1766, painting.

expressed in the sorrowful Portuguese singing known as *fado*,
which began to be heard on its streets from the 1820s. As Dickens
noticed on his visit in the 1850s, for all the colour, charm and
exuberance of the city's street life, the 'common people' of Lisbon
never seemed to laugh.[16]

Sailors go to the aid of survivors of the earthquake in Messina, Italy, 1908,
as shown in the *Le Petit Journal* newspaper.

3 Seismology Begins

As a fledgling science, seismology dates from the mid-eighteenth century. This was the period of the earthquakes in London and the subsequent Royal Society reports; the 1755 earthquake in Lisbon and the Portuguese government questionnaire answered by affected parishes; and, in particular, the geological paper by the astronomer John Michell published by the Royal Society in 1760. Michell, as mentioned, correctly identified the wave motion involved in earthquakes. The same idea was proposed, if less articulately, by an astronomer on the other side of the Atlantic, John Winthrop IV of Harvard University, after he saw the bricks in his chimney in Boston move in an undulation – rising up in sequence, then quickly dropping back into place – following an undersea earthquake off Cape Ann, north of Massachusetts Bay, in 1755. Winthrop described the motion as 'one small *wave of earth* rolling along'.[1] However, Michell's and Winthrop's early insights would lie dormant in the world of science until the mid-nineteenth century.

During the intervening period the world's first touring earthquake commission was appointed as a result of six disastrous quakes in Calabria, the 'toe' of Italy south of Naples, in February and March 1783. These claimed some 35,000 lives – including six members of the family of the Neapolitan secretary of war – and were massively destructive. But unusually, the destruction was localized: some towns were flattened while neighbouring towns escaped with only light damage. This variation in the levels of destructiveness provided investigators with valuable data that permitted the first attempts to measure and compare earthquakes.

The secretary of war toured the stricken area and noted that the biggest of the six earthquakes, on 28 March, which was also the last in the series, was nevertheless not the most lethal. A possible explanation, he thought, was that by this time the inhabitants of the region, terrified by the earlier deaths and destruction, had moved out of doors, away from buildings. Following in his footsteps, the Academy of Sciences and Fine Letters of the kingdom of Naples surveyed more than 150 towns and villages. Its 372-page report, containing maps and drawings, tabulated the time of each earthquake, the number of fatalities and the level of damage, any aftershocks and sea waves, the impact on survivors and any subsequent epidemics, as well as describing the geology of the area.

No theory of earthquakes emerged from this report, but it did lead to the creation of the first intensity scale for earthquakes: the earliest effort to quantify the phenomenon. The scale was the work of an Italian physician, Domenico Pignataro. He reviewed

Earthquake destruction, Reggio di Calabria, Italy, 1783.

Robert Mallet
(1810–1881),
pioneering
seismologist.

accounts of earthquakes in Italy – 1,181 in all – during the period
from 1 January 1783 to 1 October 1786. He categorized them
according to their number of fatalities and their level of damage,
as 'slight', 'moderate', 'strong' and 'very strong' – except for the
Calabrian earthquakes, which he judged to be 'violent'.

It was a rough-and-ready beginning to earthquake measurement. Refinement had to await the occurrence of another
devastating shock, in an area closer to Naples, in mid-December
1857, which was then supposed to be the third greatest European
earthquake ever recorded. When the news reached Britain it
immediately attracted the attention of a brilliant Irish civil engineer, Robert Mallet, who was also a Fellow of the Royal Society.
Mallet had first become interested in earthquakes in 1830 after
seeing a diagram in a book showing how the upper sections of

two stone pillars in Calabria had been twisted by an earthquake, leaving the pillars still standing. Having attempted to explain the natural forces involved in such a distortion without finding a satisfactory solution, Mallet was soon fascinated by earthquakes. Over twenty years he collected as much data about historical quakes as possible. His catalogue of world seismicity contained 6,831 listings, giving the date, location, number of shocks and probable direction and duration of the seismic waves, along with notes on related effects. In 1851 Mallet also experimented with artificial earthquakes by exploding underground charges of dynamite. He used a stopwatch to time the period between the explosion and the ripples created on the surface of a container of mercury. An illuminated image of crosshairs was projected on the mercury and its reflection viewed through an 11-power magnifier; the slight shaking in the mercury caused by the 'earthquake' made the reflected image blur or disappear. This proto-seismometer gave Mallet the speed of earthquake waves passing through different kinds of material: about twice as fast through granite as through sandy soil, he calculated. However, the speeds were much lower than they should have been – indeed, lower than Mallet himself expected – possibly because his seismometer failed to detect the earliest arrival of waves.

Less than a fortnight after the earthquake of 1857, Mallet appealed to the Royal Society for a grant to cover part of the cost of examining the affected area of the kingdom of Naples. 'Within the last 10 years only', he told the president of the society, 'seismology has taken its place in cosmic science.'[2] Here was a great opportunity to advance the newcomer. A grant of £150 was promptly forthcoming, and Mallet's investigation began in January 1858. As he later reported:

> When the observer first enters upon one of those earthquake-shaken towns, he finds himself in the midst of utter confusion. The eye is bewildered by 'a city become a heap'. He wanders over masses of dislocated stone and mortar, with timbers half buried, prostrate, or standing stark up against the light, and is appalled by spectacles of desolation ...

At first sight, and even after cursory examination, all appears confusion. Houses seem to have been precipitated to the ground in every direction of azimuth. There seems no governing law, nor any indication of a prevailing direction of overturning force. It is only by first gaining some commanding point, whence a general view over the whole field of ruin can be had, and observing its places of greatest and least destruction, and then by patient examination, compass in hand, of many details of overthrow, house by house and street by street, analyzing each detail and comparing, as to the direction of force, that must have produced each particular fall, with those previously observed and compared, that we at length perceive, once [and] for all, that this apparent confusion is but superficial.[3]

Assessing every crack of the damage with a trained eye, Mallet compiled isoseismal maps: that is, maps with contours of equal earthquake damage/intensity (a method employed today, with refinements, to map seismic hazard). Although he placed too much reliance on the direction of fallen objects and the type of cracks in buildings as indicators of earthquake motion – cracking

Map of the seismic bands of the Mediterranean by Robert Mallet, 1862.

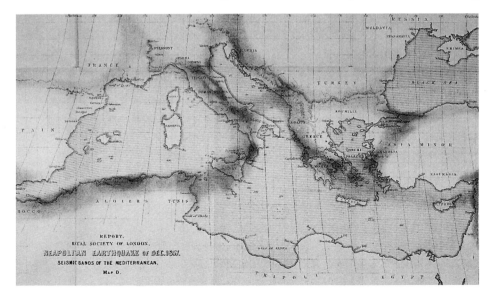

is in fact mainly a function of the type of building construction – Mallet's maps allowed him to estimate the centre of the shaking and the relative size of the earthquake. Using the new technique of photography, he documented the damage. He then reported at length to the Royal Society in a two-volume study, *Great Neapolitan Earthquake of 1857: The First Principles of Observational Seismology*, published in 1862. Elsewhere, he also published maps of world seismic intensity, providing the first indication that earthquakes cluster in certain belts around the earth. An explanation of why this is so, involving plate tectonics, would not come for another century, but in the meantime Mallet's map focused the attention of science on the puzzling patterns.

The intensity of an earthquake is not be confused with its magnitude, the figure generally reported in newspapers. Both measure the size of a quake, but whereas magnitude is calculated from the vibration of a pendulum in a seismograph, intensity is based on visible damage to structures built by humans, changes in the earth's surface such as fissures, and first-hand reports: for example, the effects on a person driving a car at the time. Intensity measures what human beings perceive as a result of an earthquake; magnitude, what scientific instruments detect.

The particular intensity scale normally used today – there are several others in use – is a modified form of that created by the Italian volcanologist Giuseppe Mercalli in 1902. It has major drawbacks. A glance will show the subjective nature of a measurement, and that it depends on building construction quality, which cannot be easily assessed: one house may remain standing in an earthquake, for instance, while the one next door fails. The scale is also culturally dependent: an intensity indicator useful in one context may be useless in another. Damage to stone and reinforced concrete buildings is important in, say, Tokyo, but scarcely relevant in an Indian village. In fact, Californian earthquake scientists have suggested modifying Mercalli's scale for California so as to include the level of disturbance in grocery, liquor and furniture stores, and even the motion induced in waterbeds! Finally, and least satisfactorily, the Mercalli scale takes no account at all of the observer's distance from the epicentre:

MODIFIED MERCALLI INTENSITY SCALE OF 1931

I Not felt except by a very few under especially favourable circumstances.

II Felt only by a few persons at rest, especially on upper floors of buildings. Delicately suspended objects may swing.

III Felt quite noticeably indoors, especially on upper floors of buildings, but many people do not recognize it as an earthquake. Standing motor cars may rock slightly. Vibration like passing of truck. Duration estimated.

IV During the day felt indoors by many, outdoors by few. At night some awakened. Dishes, windows, doors disturbed; walls make cracking sound. Sensation like heavy truck striking building. Standing motor cars rocked noticeably.

V Felt by nearly everyone, many awakened. Some dishes, windows etc., broken; a few instances of cracked plaster; unstable objects overturned. Disturbances of trees, poles and other tall objects sometimes noticed. Pendulum clocks may stop.

VI Felt by all, many frightened and run outdoors. Some heavy furniture moved; a few instances of fallen plaster or damaged chimneys. Damage slight.

VII Everybody runs outdoors. Damage negligible in buildings of good design and construction; slight to moderate in well-built ordinary structures; considerable in poorly built or badly designed structures; some chimneys broken. Noticed by persons driving motor cars.

VIII Damage slight in specially designed structures; considerable in ordinary substantial buildings, with partial collapse; great in poorly built structures. Panel walls thrown out of frame structures. Fall of chimneys, factory stacks, columns, monuments, walls. Heavy furniture overturned. Sand and mud ejected in small amounts. Changes in well water. Persons driving motor cars disturbed.

IX Damage considerable in specially designed structures; well-designed frame structures thrown out of plumb; great in substantial buildings, with partial collapse. Buildings shifted off foundations. Ground cracked conspicuously. Underground pipes broken.

X Some well-built wooden structures destroyed; most masonry and frame structures destroyed with foundations; ground badly cracked. Rails bent. Landslides considerable from river banks and steep slopes. Shifted sand and mud. Water splashed (slopped) over banks.

XI Few, if any, (masonry) structures remain standing. Bridges destroyed. Broad fissures in ground. Underground pipelines completely out of service. Earth slumps and land slips in soft ground. Rails bent greatly.

XII Damage total. Practically all works of construction are damaged greatly or destroyed. Waves seen on ground surface. Lines of sight and level are distorted. Objects are thrown upward into the air.

Mercalli Intensity Scale, updated version of 1931.

a small earthquake close by the observer can register a higher intensity than a large one far away from him.

Still, intensity scales are extremely useful. Many areas of the world lack seismographs capable of measuring the ground motion in strong earthquakes. Also, the seismic record before the twentieth century consists only of intensity reports. Intensity is thus the only quantitative way to compare a pre-twentieth-century earthquake with a modern one.

After Mallet's work deeper understanding of earthquakes, including the measurement of their magnitudes, required the

La dolorosa fine d'uno scienziato: il direttore dell'Osservatorio vesuviano, prof. Mercalli, bruciato vivo nel suo studio, a Napoli.

(Disegno di A. Beltrame)

Death of the volcanologist and seismologist Giuseppe Mercalli (1850–1914)
in his laboratory, by Achille Beltrame, 1914.

Essentials of the
seismograph.

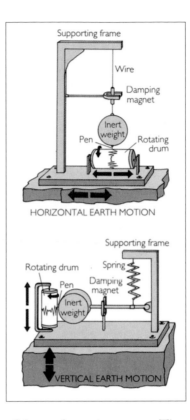

development of the modern seismometer. The essential element
in all seismometers is a frame from which is freely suspended a
mass – a pendulum – which either swings from side to side or
oscillates up and down on a spring. The swinging mass responds
to the transverse, horizontal motions of the ground; the oscillating
mass to the vertical ground motions. The inertia of the suspended mass makes it lag behind, rather than coincide with, the
movement of the frame, which naturally follows the shaking of
the ground: the mechanism of the seismometer permits this relative motion of the mass and the ground to be recorded. If the
movement of the mass is so arranged as to record a trace on a roll
of uniformly moving paper, or nowadays a digital trace on a
computer, then the seismometer is known as a seismograph.

The earliest seismometer dates back two millennia, to ancient
China. It was invented in AD 132 by the astronomer and math-

ematician Zhang Heng, also known as Choko and Tyoko (modifications of the Japanese form of his Chinese name). His device consisted of eight dragon-heads facing the eight principal directions of the compass. They were mounted on the outside of an ornamented vessel said to resemble a wine jar approximately 2 metres (6 feet) in diameter. Around the vessel's base, directly beneath the dragon-heads, were eight squatting toads with open mouths. In the event of an earthquake a bronze ball would drop from a dragon-head into a toad's mouth with a resonant clang; the direction of the earthquake was probably indicated by which dragon-head dropped its ball, unless more than one ball dropped, indicating a more complex shaking.

The mechanism inside Zhang Heng's seismometer is unknown. Seismologists of the nineteenth and twentieth centuries therefore speculated on it and even built working models of it. Whatever its precise arrangement, the mechanism must have comprised a pendulum of some kind as the primary sensing element, somehow connected to lever devices that caused the bronze balls to drop.

At any rate, according to a Chinese history, *Gokanjo* (History of the Later Han), in AD 138 the seismometer is said to have enabled Zhang Heng to announce the occurrence of a major earthquake at Rosei, 650 kilometres (400 miles) to the north-west of the Chinese capital, Loyang, two or three days before news of the devastation arrived via messengers on galloping horses. This prediction apparently restored the faith of those who had doubted the efficacy of the seismometer, and led the imperial government to appoint a secretary to monitor the behaviour of the instrument, which remained in existence for four centuries.

The first seismometer intended to record the relative displacement of the ground and a pendulum bob was built in 1751 in Italy by Andrea Bina. However, it used a pointer attached to the swinging bob so as to leave a trace in a static bed of sand, and there is no record of its actually being used to measure an earthquake. Other seismometers, including Mallet's mercury-based instrument, followed during the next century. However, the earliest modern seismograph – that is, an instrument capable of

The astronomer Zhang Heng (AD 78–139) with his dragon-head seismometer, as depicted by a 19th-century Chinese artist.

recording both horizontal and vertical motions with a timed trace on a moving surface – did not arrive until 1875. Invented by another Italian, the seismologist P. F. Cecchi, it introduced the idea of using two swinging pendulums to measure horizontal motions at right angles to each other and an oscillating pendulum on a spring to measure vertical motion. But it was insensitive and was scarcely used; indeed, the earliest surviving seismogram from a Cecchi seismograph dates only from 1887. During the 1880s it was superseded by exciting seismographic developments in Japan. 'Cecchi's seismograph notwithstanding,' note two historians of early seismometry, James Dewey and Perry Byerly,

> it seems clear to us that the credit for the introduction of the seismograph in seismology belongs to a group of British professors teaching in Japan in the late nineteenth century. These scientists obtained the first known records of ground motion as a function of time. Furthermore, they knew what such records could reveal about the nature of earthquake motion. They used their instruments to study the propagation of seismic waves, and they used them to study, for engineering purposes, the behaviour of the ground in earthquakes.[4]

Around 1870, as Meiji Japan rapidly opened itself to the West, the Japanese government began to hire foreign staff in scientific and technical positions in its new ministries and as teachers at the newly created Imperial College of Technology in Tokyo (which became part of the Tokyo Imperial University in 1886). Between 1865 and 1900 somewhere between 2,000 and 5,000 Western experts – mostly in their twenties – went to work in Japan. Officially known as *oyatoi-gaikokujin* – which literally means 'honourable foreign menials or hirelings' – they were intended to help modernize Japan without being given any positions of real power that might relegate the strongly national-istic Japanese to the status of colonial subjects.

Ironically, seismology was not one of the areas in which the foreigners were invited to work. The Japanese were so accus-tomed to the shaking of the earth that they felt no urgency to study earthquakes. Foreigners living in Japan, however, were acutely aware of the unfamiliar phenomenon. At the Imperial College of Technology earthquakes were a constant subject of conversation among the expatriate teachers in the 1870s. 'We had earthquakes for breakfast, dinner, tea and supper', said one of them, John Milne.[5] As a result seismology in Japan was founded not by the Japanese but by foreign professors from

Front page of the *Daily Mirror* announcing the death of seismologist John Milne (1850–1913). Milne's Japanese wife is shown on the left.

The Daily Mirror

THE MORNING JOURNAL WITH THE SECOND LARGEST NET SALE

No. 3,049.   FRIDAY, AUGUST 1, 1913   One Halfpenny.

DEATH OF PROFESSOR JOHN MILNE, THE FAMOUS ENGLISH INVENTOR OF INSTRUMENTS TO DETECT EARTHQUAKES AND REGISTER THEIR MOVEMENTS.

related disciplines, such as geology, mining and civil engineering, most of whom came from Britain. Eventually, in 1886, the world's first chair in seismology was established at the Tokyo Imperial University and filled by a protégé of Milne, Sekiya Seikei. Other notable Japanese seismologists, such as Fusakichi Omori, appeared before the turn of the century when Japan was for a brief period the world leader in seismological science, with its epicentre at the Tokyo Imperial University. Surprisingly, the United States had no teaching course in seismology until as late as 1911, five years after the great San Francisco earthquake, when a course was introduced at the University of California under the disguise of geology.

Milne was the most significant of these foreign professors in Japan. He came to Tokyo from England in 1876, at the age of 26, as a professor of mining and geology; married a Japanese woman (the daughter of a Buddhist abbot) in the 1880s; and lived in Japan until 1895 – a period much longer than most *oyatoi gaikokujin*. In 1880, following a sharp earthquake in Tokyo-Yokohama, Milne urged the founding of the Seismological Society of Japan – the first body in the world devoted to seismology – headed, at Milne's insistence, by a Japanese. His seismograph, designed in 1881 with two other British scientists (James Ewing and Thomas Gray) and employed at the college in Tokyo, was widely deployed in Japan, beginning in 1883, when one was manufactured in Glasgow and presented to the Meiji Emperor by the British Association for the Advancement of Science. After he returned to Britain in 1895, Milne was largely responsible for establishing a network of seismographic stations throughout the world. These collected data for evaluation at a central observatory run by himself, located at his home at Shide on the Isle of Wight. This record was then published to an international audience in 'The Shide Circular Reports on Earthquakes', issued from 1900 until 1912, the year before Milne died. He also wrote a classic textbook on seismology. Although his theoretical contributions to the subject were small, Milne has a considerable claim to be considered the founder of seismology.[6]

The earthquake of 1880 opened up a split unique to Japan: between advocates of traditional Japanese buildings constructed in wood, and advocates of modern Western architecture built in brick and stone. Japanese buildings were relatively immune from earthquakes, though prone to fire, whereas Western-style buildings were prone to collapse in earthquakes, though relatively immune from fires. In the 1870s, after the annihilation of part of Tokyo in a fire, the modernizing government had constructed in brick a showpiece residential and shopping area, the Ginza, designed by an Irish architect; but despite being fireproof, the Ginza had failed to attract residents and businesses, to the embarrassment of the government. Expensive rents, inconvenience and the unfamiliarity of the Ginza's layout and appearance played a part in this indifference, but so, too, it appears, did the fear of being caught in a Western-style building during an earthquake. Thus, during the construction of a new Imperial Palace beginning in 1879, the wholly Western-style design had to be modified as a result of cracking during a minor earthquake. While the ministerial offices in the new palace continued to be built in brick, the residence of the emperor was switched to a wooden construction, and was designed by the official carpenter to the imperial court rather than the original foreign architect. Obviously, there was more to this debate over Japanese versus Western construction than simply engineering considerations. Milne soon found himself in the thick of it.

He was keen to record the damage caused by the Tokyo-Yokohama earthquake of 1880 and compare it with the damage recorded by Mallet after the Neapolitan earthquake of 1857. But few Japanese buildings in Tokyo demonstrated the data that Milne required. With some regret, he observed:

> Everywhere the houses are built of wood and generally speaking are so flexible that although at the time of a shock they swing violently from side to side in a manner which would result in utter destruction to a house of brick or stone, when the shock is over, by the stiffness of their joints, they return to their original position, and leave no trace which gives us any definite information about the nature of the movement which has taken place.[7]

Indeed, some Japanese buildings, such as pagodas, had long used elaborate wooden roof jointing explicitly to protect against earthquake damage.

The brick and stone buildings of Yokohama, by happy contrast (at least for Milne), acted as 'one great seismometer'. Nearly all of the city's brick-built chimneys collapsed in 1880, along with a few of its Western-style houses – but not one of its Japanese houses was much damaged, as in Tokyo, except for some warehouses that lost a little plaster. In Yokohama Milne therefore sent out questionnaires to the foreign residents requesting them to report on the damage, for example whether their windows had broken and at what time, and the direction of fall of their chimneys. In Tokyo he had to resort to examining the only bits of masonry that were widely available: gravestones in the countryside around the city, which had toppled during the earthquake in revealing ways. 'What consolation the residents in Yokohama may have received for the losses they have received, I am unable to say,' he wrote, 'but certainly if the houses in which they dwell had not been built our information about this earthquake would have been so small as to be almost valueless.'

During the 1880s Milne developed a system of monitoring earthquakes throughout Japan with the help of meteorologists, telegraph operators, the military and the state bureaucracy. Beginning at home, so to speak, he turned the Tokyo Imperial University's main building into a seismometer by tagging, dating and measuring existing cracks in its foundations and attaching devices similar to seismographs directly to its walls. In 1882 he started to send out bundles of postcards to local government offices, such as post offices and schools, requesting a bureaucrat to mail a postcard to him in Tokyo every week recording the number of shocks he had felt. Having thereby established the areas of most frequent seismic activity, Milne then sited in these areas clocks that were designed to stop when sufficiently shaken, thus providing comparable reports on the timing of earthquakes in different places. In 1883 precise instructions on how to keep these time records were issued to civil servants by the Seismological Society's Committee on a System of Earthquake Observations. Some of the clocks were placed in the field stations of the Imperial Meteorological Observatory. In the end Milne 'successfully piggy-backed seismic monitoring onto the existing tasks of a host of government functionaries'.[8]

In 1891 Milne finally experienced a devastating Japanese earthquake to rival the one in Italy investigated by Mallet in 1857. It occurred in the alluvial Nobi Plain, known as 'the garden of Japan', and is today called the Great Nobi earthquake or, more commonly, the Mino-Owari earthquake. Its shockwaves were felt throughout almost all of Japan. Magnitude scales were yet to be invented but, on the evidence of contemporary seismograms, the magnitude may have been as high as 8.4, making the Mino-Owari earthquake as severe as the Great Kanto earthquake of 1923, or slightly more so. With about 7,300 fatalities, tens of thousands of injuries and more than 100,000 people made homeless, this earthquake was the largest in Japan since the 1855 quake that had destroyed Edo (Tokyo).

As for the damage, Milne reported to the British Association in 1892:

> If we may judge from the contortions produced along lines of railway, the fissuring of the ground, the destruction of hundreds of miles of high embankments which guard the plains from river-floods, the utter ruin of structures of all descriptions, the sliding down of mountain sides and the toppling over of their peaks, the compression of valleys and other bewildering phenomena, we may confidently say that

Damage to railway tracks following the Mino-Owari earthquake, Japan, 1891.

last year, on the morning of 28 October, Central Japan received as terrible a shaking as has ever been recorded in the history of seismology.[9]

The following year he and a fellow engineer at the Tokyo Imperial University, William Burton, proved the truth of this report by publishing a book in Japan, *The Great Earthquake of Japan 1891*, with a plate section of startling photographs of twisted railway lines, broken bridges and ruined factories. At the same time Milne also joined the government's Imperial Earthquake Investigation Committee, formed as a direct result of the earthquake. He was the only foreigner to be invited to serve alongside Japanese engineers, architects, seismologists, geologists, mathematicians and physicists from the Tokyo Imperial University. The committee was the first official Japanese organization to plan for the effects of future earthquakes.

Around this time, however, seismology took an international turn with the invention of more sensitive seismographs in Europe. These used optical, rather than mechanical, recording on a continuously moving photographic surface. From now on earthquakes could increasingly be studied in seismological laboratories on the other side of the planet from their epicentres. In 1889 a seismograph located in Potsdam, Germany, designed by Ernst von Rebeur-Paschwitz, detected a large earthquake about an hour after it was felt in Japan. Milne confirmed the truth of this observation, and in 1894 went on to design a new seismograph using photographic recording that carried his name. Its sensitivity may have played a part in his decision to leave Japan in 1895 and return to Britain, since he realized that he could now continue to study Japanese earthquakes from there. Another factor, however, is that he had had the misfortune to lose his entire house in Tokyo in a fire.

As for Japanese seismologists, they began to travel outside Japan, especially after Japan's success in the Russo–Japanese War of 1904–5. In 1905 Omori went to India with a group of scientists and architects to record the aftershocks of a major earthquake in Assam. In 1906 he travelled to California after the famous

previous pages: Damage to the Nagara Gawa railway bridge after the Mino-Owari earthquake, 1891.

Seismologist
Fusakichi Omori
(1868–1923) depicted
in the *San Francisco
Call* (August 1906).

earthquake, examined the ruins of San Francisco (where he was
attacked and slightly injured by some anti-Japanese survivors)
and wrote a report, which was the first detailed account of the
earthquake to reach European scientists. A local newspaper carried a large photograph of Omori under the headline 'World's
Greatest Seismologist Says San Francisco Is Safe'.[10] And in
1908 he investigated the appalling southern Italian earthquake
in Messina in which 120,000 people died (see p. 52). There he
concluded that the much smaller Japanese fatality figure in the
Mino-Owari earthquake of 1891 would undoubtedly have been
far greater if ordinary Japanese homes were built of brick and
stone, as in Italy, rather than of wood.

At the same time geologists and physicists, such as William
Thomson, Lord Kelvin, began to understand the new potential

of seismology to provide 'X-rays' of the inner structure of the earth. It could do this through calculating the speeds and trajectories of seismic waves as they passed via different regions of the crust, mantle and core and were detected by distant seismographs. During the early twentieth century seismology would increasingly be seen as part of the broad-ranging subject known as geophysics. But it still lacked any kind of a universal theory of where, when and why earthquakes occur. Omori's predictions concerning future earthquakes in the Tokyo region would turn out, as we shall see, to be disastrously wrong.

4 Tokyo, 1923: Holocaust

Before the Great Kanto earthquake of September 1923, the most serious earthquakes to ravage Edo (Tokyo) were those of 1703 and 1855. The first of these claimed around 2,300 lives, and an estimated 100,000 further lives in the tsunami produced by the earthquake. The second, known as the Ansei earthquake, provoked the popular outpouring of catfish prints (*namazu-e*) mentioned in chapter One. Although its magnitude has been estimated as comparatively low, between 6.9 and 7.1, its shallow focus and epicentre near the heart of the city caused substantial fatalities and property damage, mainly from fire: between 7,000 and 10,000 people died in and around Edo, and at least 14,000 structures were destroyed. Multiple aftershocks, as many as 80 per day, continued for nine days after the earthquake.

However, in the long run, the psychological effects of the Ansei earthquake of 1855 were more important than its physical ones. The quake struck the capital at a time of political stagnation in Japan's ruling class, the late Tokugawa shogunate, and one that was ominously close to the two visits in 1853 and 1854 of the American naval officer Commodore Matthew Perry and his steamship squadron – a famous example of gunboat diplomacy which began the opening of isolationist Japan to Western trade and influence. Certain of the catfish prints of 1855 even link the earthquake directly to Perry's visit in their images and captions, encapsulating the ambivalent mixture of rejection and fascination in the Japanese reaction towards the American intruders.

In one print, for example, the *namazu* has morphed into a threatening black whale spouting coins – not from its blowhole but rather from the place where a smoke stack is located on a steamship. Thus the whale is intended to resemble one of Perry's 'black ships'. Japanese people standing on the shore beckon the wealth-creating whale-*namazu* to come closer. In another print two figures – a kneeling *namazu* (with a builder's trowel near its tail) and Commodore Perry (with a rifle near his feet) – literally engage in a neck-to-neck tug-of-war, judged by a Japanese referee. Victory is going to neither side, but the catfish seems to have the edge over the American officer, who has been dragged slightly forward as the referee hails the fish. An extensive accompanying text contains a dialogue between the *namazu* and Perry that contrasts an aggressive America, effectively governed, with a Japan whose ineffective feudal government means that its people must turn for help to benevolent deities (such as Kashima, the controller of the *namazu*). Even the earthquake-causing *namazu* is seen as partly beneficial. 'For Edo residents, the earthquake

Namazu (catfish) fights Commodore Perry, following the Ansei earthquake of 1855, woodblock print.

Namazu depicted as a whale/steamship, following the Ansei earthquake of 1855, woodblock print.

76

of 1855 was an act of *yonaoshi*, or "world rectification"', writes the American scholar Gregory Smits. 'In this view, the Ansei earthquake literally shook up a society that had grown complacent, imbalanced, and sick.'[1] Although it would be too much to say that the Ansei earthquake was principally responsible for the social discontent and ensuing modernizing movement in Japan that eventually overthrew the shogunate and led to the restoration of the Meiji emperor in 1868, it undoubtedly played a major role, particularly through the subversive messages contained in the *namazu-e*. 'The anonymous print makers of Edo posited that the earthquake under their city had shaken up all of Japan, and they were right', Smits concludes.[2]

For the recently created science of seismology the leading question in Japan at the turn of the century was, inevitably: when would Tokyo suffer again from another great earthquake? In 1905 this issue, writes Gregory Clancey in *Earthquake Nation: The Cultural Politics of Japanese Seismicity*, created 'a rift, which remains legendary among contemporary Japanese seismologists', between Fusakichi Omori, professor of seismology at the Tokyo Imperial University, and his colleague Akitsune Imamura, the assistant professor.[3] Although junior to Omori in position, Imamura was only marginally younger than him, and the two men quickly became rivals.

In Omori's opinion the risk to Tokyo was reduced, not enhanced, by the frequent seismic activity on geological faults beneath the capital, since he thought that smaller earthquakes released the potentially dangerous build-up of seismic stress. Instead, his suspicions focused on areas where there had been long gaps in seismic activity, such as the Nobi Plain, which had been comparatively quiet for hundreds of years before the terrible Mino-Owari earthquake of 1891. Imamura, by contrast, focused on Sagami Bay, south of Tokyo, where the fact that the geological faults were underwater meant that there was a disturbing absence of seismic records. In an article for a popular journal in 1905 Imamura went so far as to predict that there would be a great earthquake in Tokyo within 50 years and advised that the city should be ready for a worst-case scenario. Moreover, he argued that given Tokyo's largely wooden construction, a great earthquake would cause a fire with in excess of 100,000 casualties.

Despite its prescience, Imamura's 1905 prediction had no scientific evidence to support it. Omori therefore publicly denounced Imamura's idea in an article in the same journal, entitled 'Rumours of Tokyo and a Great Earthquake', comparing the apocalyptic prediction with a popular 'fire horse' legend that conflagrations would occur during years in which there was an alignment of the astrological symbols for 'fire' and 'horse'. 'The theory that a large earthquake will take place in Tokyo in the near future is academically baseless and trivial', Omori asserted.[4] But Imamura refused to back down, although he was now shunned by some of his scientific colleagues. In 1915 the two seismologists once more clashed publicly over the prediction. This time Imamura had to leave his position at the Tokyo Imperial University for a while; when he returned to his home village, even his father censured him.

Omori's reputation, meanwhile, increased. His design of a seismograph, known as the Bosch-Omori seismograph (Bosch after its German manufacturer), was widely used throughout the world in the early twentieth century. Not only was Omori hailed as a great seismologist in far-off San Francisco, he also made predictions of earthquakes around the Pacific rim, in southern Italy and in China that appeared to be borne out by seismic events in the Aleutians and in Valparaíso in 1906, in Messina in 1908, in Avezzano in 1915 and in Kansu in 1920 – although it should be emphasized that Omori predicted the locations, not the timings, of these earthquakes. In his native Japan, however, Omori's theory of seismic gaps and release of seismic stress would now turn out to be a terrible failure.

In late 1921 the strongest earthquake in Tokyo for 28 years damaged a conduit and almost cut off the city from its water supply. An even stronger one in mid-1922 damaged buildings, cut the phone service and stopped the railways. Then, in early 1923, there was a third shock, less severe than the previous two.

Following his theory, Omori believed that these shocks, especially the third one, had demonstrated the relief of seismic stress in the faults beneath Tokyo. The capital could now relax. In a scientific paper published in 1922, he speculated that 'probably the semi-destructive earthquake on 26 April 1922, has finished the activity epoch succeeding the period of the seismic rest during the last half a dozen years.'[5] The weaker shock in 1923 reinforced his conviction, and he wrote:

> Tokyo may be assumed to be free in future from the visitation of a violent earthquake like that of 1855, as the latter shock originated right under the city itself, and as destructive earthquakes do not repeat from one and the same origin, at least not in the course of 1,000 or 1,500 years.[6]

By the time this second paper appeared in print in 1924, the Great Kanto earthquake had destroyed most of Tokyo, and Omori himself was no more.

On 1 September 1923, the day of the earthquake, Omori was far away from Tokyo in Sydney, Australia, at the Second Pan-Pacific Science Conference. He was being shown a seismograph by an Australian seismologist when it suddenly sprang to life and recorded the distant destruction of his home city. Initial news reports mentioned tens of thousands of deaths, but Omori told Australian reporters that these figures were probably exaggerations – as had happened in the initial reports of 100,000 deaths in the Ansei earthquake of 1855 – before boarding the first available ship to Tokyo. The Australian journalists were not convinced. A reporter from the Melbourne newspaper *The Age* remarked that despite Japanese seismologists such as Omori having tried their best at earthquake prediction, 'the present horror is a sad commentary on their labours'.[7]

Omori's colleague and rival Imamura was at his desk in the Seismological Institute of the Tokyo Imperial University when the shaking began. He later described the experience:

> At first, the movement was rather slow and feeble so that I did not take it to be the forerunner of so big a shock. As usual, I began to estimate the duration of the preliminary

Seismogram of
1 September 1923
from the University
of Tokyo (then Tokyo
Imperial University)
showing the initial
shock waves from
the Great Kanto
earthquake.

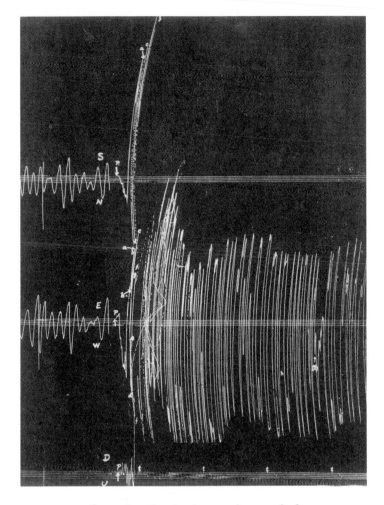

tremors. Soon the vibration became large and after 3 or
4 seconds from the commencement I felt the shock very
strongly indeed. 7 or 8 seconds passed and the house was
shaking to an extraordinary extent, but I considered these
movements not yet to be the principal portion . . . The
motion went on to increase in intensity very quickly, and
after 4 or 5 seconds I felt it to have reached its strongest.
During this epoch, the tiles were showering down from
the roof making a loud noise, and I wondered whether the
building could stand or not.[8]

Soon after this the Institute's seismographs were overturned by the shaking, though not before registering the initial vibrations reported by Imamura, and the walls of the university building began to collapse. Imamura and colleagues became firefighters, without water or help from outside, as they desperately attempted to save from incineration the seismological records of half a century, going back to the days of their British predecessors Ewing, Gray and Milne.

Imamura survived the earthquake unscathed. Whether by luck or good judgement, he had the grim satisfaction of seeing his prediction of 1905 come true – not only in the timing of the earthquake (well within his 50-year window) and the scale of the disaster (well over 100,000 deaths from fire) but in its location, too, with the epicentre under Sagami Bay. He also, thanks to Omori's chance absence in Australia, became a crucial scientific adviser to the Japanese government and a leading spokesman to the world's press. Greeting his senior colleague at the devastated dockside on Omori's return from Australia, Imamura reportedly had the satisfaction of receiving an apology. But by then Omori was a sick man, suffering from a brain tumour. He died in a Tokyo hospital some two months after the earthquake, at the age

Map of Sagami Bay, Japan, showing the epicentre of the Great Kanto earthquake, 1923.

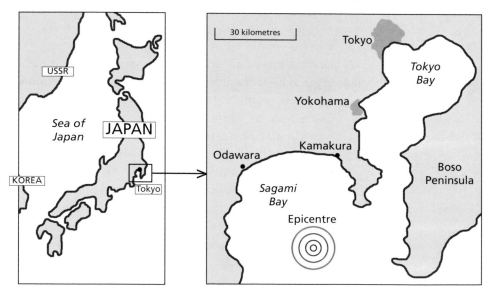

of only 55. 'It was the end of a life and career hardly capable of continuing as before', concludes Clancey in his compelling account of the Omori–Imamura dispute.[9] It was also a foretaste of the bitter, unresolvable controversies that would surround earthquake prediction in Japan, the United States, Italy and every other 'earthquake nation' throughout the rest of the century and up to the present day.

The shock waves radiating from beneath the ocean floor of Sagami Bay struck Yokohama first, at exactly 11.58 a.m. They hit Tokyo a little further from the epicentre towards the northeast, 44 seconds after Yokohama. As in Lisbon in 1755 and in Edo in 1855, the aftershocks continued through day and night over several days. At the Tokyo Imperial University Imamura detected more than 171 aftershocks between 11.58 a.m. and 6 p.m., and a further 51 before midnight on 1 September.

Noboru Oshima, a reporter for the Jiji news agency in Yokohama, was lucky. He was in the office at 11.58 a.m. when he heard a sound 'like a distant detonation'.[10] The next moment, he and his chair were tossed well above the floor and then landed face down on the ground. The building was swaying violently and groaning in a sinister manner, but somehow Oshima got to the head of the stairs. He was promptly thrown down them, rolling down head first. 'I was up in an instant and leapt out of the building, only to fall 3 feet into a fissure which the shaking had made in the concrete sidewalk', he reported. When he managed to get to his feet and look around, he saw that every house, so far as the eye could see through the brown-black sky swirling with clouds of dust and smoke, had collapsed. 'The foreign houses on the bluff were already afire, sending up black smoke columns. The people in the street were all tottering.'

In Tokyo Randall Gould, a reporter with the *Japan Times*, was similarly fortunate. He was about to eat a sandwich lunch when the shaking started. 'Most of the office came down,' he said, 'but not all of it.'[11] Grabbing his typewriter, he scrambled into the street, where he saw that few other buildings were left standing. The city's trams had stopped in their tracks. At the Akasaka Palace, where the prince regent, Hirohito, was eating his lunch, there was little damage because the palace was bolted onto massive concrete foundations. The prince ran into the extensive gardens, where he saw column after column of black smoke rising from the fires already burning in the city. They would continue to burn for more than 40 hours.

Immediately the people of Tokyo – with centuries of experience of great fires – headed for the open spaces in the city. The flames pushed some of them back towards the Imperial Palace. Caught between certain death by fire and an armed confrontation with the police guarding the palace, the crowds forced their way into the safety of the palace's outer gardens and encamped there for several days. Others fled east towards the Sumida River, hoping to reach the supposed safety of the opposite bank. But the Eitai Bridge had been almost entirely wrecked by the earthquake, leaving only a single iron beam spanning the river, high above the water. There was no choice for the refugees but to start crossing the beam in single file.

What happened next, as extracted from reports and eyewitness accounts published in the *Japan Times* during the following weeks, was a panic in hell:

> A wall of flame was now racing eastwards, fanned by the strong winds. As it began to outrun those at the rear, the crowds heading for the Eitai Bridge panicked and surged forwards, crushing and suffocating those in front and sending 50 or 60 headlong into the water.
>
> Refugees crawling, ant-like, along the iron girder looked down on a horrific scene far below. Hundreds of people were in the water, some clinging to flotsam, others drowning, many already dead. Boats worked as hard as they could to ferry survivors across, but their task was hopeless in the face of the panicking thousands who lined the bank.
>
> One survivor, a woman, later told how she was pushed into the water but managed to cling to a rope moored to the bank. As the afternoon wore on, the heat from the flames grew more intense, and she found herself having

Firestorm in Tokyo, September 1923, artist unknown.

to duck under the water every time a searing blast of wind hit her face. The river grew warm, and then frighteningly hot.[12]

At another point on the Sumida River, in the area of Nihon-bashi, the flames leapt over the water from one bank to the other – a distance of 220 metres (720 feet). Those who survived their submersion in the filthy river finally pulled themselves out, singed and blackened, on the morning of 3 September, after nearly two days without food. They had been lucky: elsewhere, in the canals of the city, many people were boiled alive.

However, the worst individual disaster by far occurred in the crowded, working-class area of Honjo. In 1920 its population was officially 256,269 people; in 1925, after the Great Kanto earthquake, the number had fallen to 207,074. (By 1940 it had risen again, to 273,407.) Some 40,000 inhabitants of Honjo perished on 1 September 1923 in one concentrated conflagration, which is still memorialized in Tokyo.

Tokyo residents take refuge on tram tracks, 1 September 1923, after the outbreak of fires following the Great Kanto earthquake.

They had taken refuge – along with the highly flammable furniture and baggage from their homes – in one of the very few open spaces in Honjo: a vacant six-hectare site that until recently had been a depot for military uniforms but at the time of the earthquake was being transformed into a park by the municipal administration. However, the space was too small to protect anyone from the raging flames that now approached it from several directions and effectively surrounded the screaming refugees. In *Tokyo: City of Stories* Paul Waley pictures the dreadful scene that transpired after sunset:

> Strong gusts of wind buffeted against the wall of flames creating a series of little whirlwinds that sucked people into the air and then dropped them down again as balls of fire. The whole park turned into a blaze of infernal proportions, hot enough to buckle steel and melt metal. Nearly everyone who had fled there was burnt to death, and afterwards the devastation was so complete that it was impossible to tell how many people had died.[13]

Of the handful who did get out, one was the eldest son of the managing director of the Tokai Bank. His father, Genjiro Yoshida, had taken his entire family to shelter in the former depot. They all died in the firestorm except for Genjiro Junior, who had a miraculous escape: he was picked up by one of the fiery whirlwinds, whisked away and then dropped in a ditch, where he somehow survived the flames.

Corpses littered downtown Tokyo, as described by the 70-year-old Akira Kurosawa in his autobiography, remembering his stunned walk through the incinerated area as a thirteen-year-old led by his elder brother. The well-known modernist writer Ryunosuke Akutagawa (author of two stories on which Kurosawa based his film *Rashomon*) also observed the aftermath in September 1923 and wrote about it only two or three years later in an autobiographical sketch, 'The Life of a Stupid Man'. Here Akutagawa describes himself (in the third person) on a visit to a pond in the red-light district of Tokyo, Yoshiwara, where hundreds of men and women – mainly courtesans – had been suffocated in a cauldron of mud:

> The odour was something close to overripe apricots. Catching a hint of it as he walked through the charred ruins, he found himself thinking such thoughts as these: *The smell of corpses rotting in the sun is not as bad as I would have expected.* When

he stood before a pond where bodies were piled upon bodies, however, he discovered that the old Chinese expression, 'burning the nose', was no mere sensory exaggeration of grief and horror. What especially moved him was the corpse of a child of 12 or 13. He felt something like envy as he looked at it, recalling such expressions as 'Those whom the gods love die young.' Both his sister and his half-brother had lost their houses to fire. His sister's husband, though, was on a suspended sentence for perjury.

Too bad we didn't all die.

Standing in the charred ruins he could hardly keep from feeling this way.[14]

This vignette was published posthumously; Akutagawa famously committed suicide in 1927 by taking an overdose of a barbiturate. His fellow writer Yasunari Kawabata, who had accompanied Akutagawa on his walk through the ruins of Tokyo, was convinced that seeing the ugly horror of the dead bodies in the pond had made Akutagawa determined to leave behind 'a handsome corpse'.[15]

Kawabata was a subtle writer who eventually became Japan's first Nobel laureate in literature. In the 1920s he wrote a fictional response to the earthquake in the form of one of his 'palm-of-the-hand' short stories, known in its English translation as 'The Money Road'. According to the beginning of the story it takes place on 1 September 1924. Its chief setting is the former military clothing depot in Honjo.

'On the anniversary of the earthquake an imperial messenger appeared at the ruins of the clothing depot', writes Kawabata.

The prime minister, the interior minister, and the mayor all read memorial addresses at the ceremony. Foreign ambassadors sent memorial wreaths.

At 11.58 all traffic stopped, and the people of the city observed a moment of silence.

Steamships that had gathered from Yokohama made the trip back and forth between Kokokashiko and the bank near

the clothing depot on the Sumida River. The automobile
companies vied to be first to make an official appearance
in front of the clothing depot. Each religious organization,
Red Cross hospital, and Christian girls school sent a relief
committee to the ceremony.

A postcard dealer rounded up some vagrants and
dispatched a squad to secretly sell photographs of bodies
mangled in the earthquake. A movie studio technician
walked around with a tall tripod. Money changers stood
in a row to change the visitors' silver coins for lesser copper
coins to be tossed into the offering box.[16]

A shrewd vagrant and beggar, Ken, dragging along an unnamed female friend – a penurious older beggar, whose entire
family was burned to death in the clothing depot – join the
crowd of mourners. She plans to offer a red comb in memory of
her dead daughter. Taking off one of his worn-out army boots,
Ken gives it to her, without explaining why, and they edge forward, walking with one bare foot and one booted foot. 'Just as
a brilliant forest of floral wreaths and funeral greenery came into
view, their feet suddenly felt cold. It was coins.' The queueing
crowd, unable to reach the offering box, had started to throw
money from wherever they stood and the coins were falling on
everyone's heads like hail. Both Ken and the woman immediately start picking up coins between their bare toes and dropping
them into the two boots. 'The closer they advanced to the charnel house on the cold money road, the deeper the layer of coins
grew. People were walking an inch off the ground.' In the end,
they excitedly hobble away in their coin-filled boots. Only then,
as they sit together on the deserted bank of the river, does the
woman remember that she forgot to offer the red comb. Empty-
ing her boot of coins, she places the comb inside it and flings
both into the river. 'The red comb floated out of the sinking boot
and silently drifted down the great river.'

In today's Tokyo there is a park on the site of the former
clothing depot in Honjo. In the middle, sheltered by trees from
the incessant traffic, stands a temple dedicated to the memory

of the victims of the fire. In the gardens around the temple stand strange, twisted sculptures, rather than the usual Japanese rock garden. Close up they can be recognized not as works of modern art but as erstwhile metal machinery, such as presses and engines, melted by the heat of the firestorms in 1923.

Opinions differ as to the historical importance of the Great Kanto earthquake – somewhat as they do about Ansei earthquake of 1855. Economically speaking, the earthquake cost Japan 40 per cent of its nominal GNP. In 1926 the government report on the earthquake noted: 'The almost total destruction of Tokyo, the capital of the Empire, and the complete destruction of Yokohama, the foremost of our leading ports, inflicted upon the nation a cruel wound and one not easy to heal.'[17] Yet a mere four

Religious service for the victims of the fire at the Honjo Military Clothing Depot, Tokyo, 1 September 1924 – the first anniversary of the Great Kanto earthquake.

The charnel house at the site of the Honjo Military Clothing Depot, Tokyo, built for the victims of the fire, 1924.

years after those words were written, in 1930, the reconstruction of Tokyo was officially complete – only for the city to suffer yet another enormous disaster in 1945, this time from American incendiary air raids.

Between 1930 and 1945, of course, came the Great Depression, the military adventurism of the Japanese government in Manchuria and the rest of China, and finally the Second World

Ruins of the 'entertainment quarters' in Asakusa Park, Tokyo, after the Great Kanto earthquake, 1923.

The Yamamoto
Cabinet meets outdoors
because of the threat
of aftershocks, Tokyo,
September 1923.

War. It is not difficult to postulate a causal connection between
the massive disruption caused by the earthquake and the eventual
declaration of total war by Japan in 1941. But it is more difficult
to substantiate such a link. Two significant books first published
in the early 1990s came up with different assessments of the
earthquake's long-term impact.

The journalist Peter Hadfield, who knows Tokyo well,
straightforwardly argues in *Sixty Seconds That Will Change the
World*, his book on 'the coming Tokyo earthquake', that the reconstruction of Tokyo provoked an economic crisis, worsened by
the Great Depression, which then allowed the complete takeover
of a military government. 'Few earthquakes in history have had
such a decisive and powerful effect on world events', writes
Hadfield.[18] By contrast, the academic Edward Seidensticker, in
Tokyo Rising: The City since the Great Earthquake, sees the earthquake's influence as more elusive. Debts arising from it played a
direct role in a financial panic in 1927 that led to the resignation
of the cabinet and the appointment of an army general as prime
minister, who advocated aggressive interventionism in China.
However, Seidensticker questions a link between this and the
subsequent militarization of Japanese society: 'Whether or not

the reaction of the thirties would have come had the depression not come, we will never know.'[19]

Instead of political influences from the earthquake, Seidensticker – who is best known as a scholar and translator of Japanese literature – discerns possible cultural influences. Before the earthquake, customers entering Tokyo department stores would automatically change their shoes for specially provided slippers; afterwards they could enter in their ordinary footwear. Japanese department stores henceforth became more like their equivalents in New York and London. At the same time, after the earthquake, Japanese women – more of whom were now working – began eating out in department-store dining rooms; before it, such public eating was not considered to be good form for a woman. Finally, the particularly Japanese passion for cartoon strips and comics with a panel narrative dates from the years immediately after the Great Kanto earthquake. 'Whether or not their origins can be blamed on the confusion that followed the earthquake, that is where they are', observes Seidensticker.[20] Given the undoubted origin of another distinctively Japanese graphic form, the *namazu-e*, in the events of the Ansei earthquake, a similar kind of cultural phenomenon after the 1923 earthquake seems plausible, if hardly earth-shaking – and also, oddly intriguing.

Damage to the John Muir School, Long Beach, near Los Angeles, following the
Long Beach earthquake, 1933.

5 Measuring Earthquakes

In human terms, earthquakes – and the tsunamis and fires that
frequently follow major quakes – can be measured by the number
of fatalities they cause, the level of injuries and how many people
they make homeless, as well as by the types of damage (such as
fissures, cracking and collapse) that they produce in land,
infrastructure and houses. We have seen all this in the great
earthquakes in Tokyo and Yokohama in 1923, near Naples in
1857, in Lisbon in 1755 and in many others. In scientific terms,
however, there are three principal ways to measure an earthquake:
by its intensity, its magnitude and its epicentre. All three measures
have been referred to many times already in this book, without
much precision. Now is the time to go into more detail about
them, and to discuss how earthquake measurement improved
during the twentieth century.

But first, a revealing story about intensity and magnitude. The
earthquake that launched the career of the world's most famous
seismologist – indeed, the only seismologist who is a household
name, the American Charles Richter – struck Long Beach near
Los Angeles in 1933. Its epicentre was offshore, southeast of
Long Beach, on a fault identified in 1920 as the Newport-
Inglewood fault. With a magnitude of 6.4 on what would soon
become known as the Richter scale, the Long Beach earthquake
killed 120 people and caused property damage estimated at $50
million in Depression-era dollars, including the collapse of several
poorly constructed schools. Only the lateness of the hour – just
before 6 p.m. on 10 March – saved hundreds of schoolchildren

from almost certain death. Within a month the state of California introduced strict design and construction regulations for public schools – the beginning of a more widespread code for earth-quake-resistant building design in California.

One witness of the earthquake was Albert Einstein, then a visiting professor at the California Institute of Technology in Pasadena about 50 kilometres (30 miles) from Long Beach. By 1933 Caltech was a major centre for seismology. Just before 6 p.m., Einstein was walking across the campus after a physics seminar, chatting mostly about earthquakes with Caltech's leading seismologist, fellow German-Jewish refugee Beno Gutenberg. Another professor approached them and asked: 'Well, what do you think of the earthquake?' 'What earthquake?' came the reply.[1] Engrossed in their conversation, the pair of scientists had failed to notice that tree branches and power lines were swaying around them. In fairness to them, the ground on which they were walking remained relatively steady in Pasadena, as compared with Long Beach, which was nearer the epicentre. When Gutenberg reached the Seismological Laboratory soon afterwards, he recounted the story to his younger colleague Richter with considerable amusement. On returning home late that night, Richter's wife told him that during the earthquake their cat had 'spat on the floor because it wasn't behaving properly'.[2] It was during this period that Richter devised and began to use his magnitude scale.

The swaying of tree branches and power lines – and perhaps the abnormal behaviour of cats and many other animals – are possible general indicators of earthquake intensity, along with all the other indicators specified in intensity scales such as the Modified Mercalli Scale. But they are clearly subjective: dependent on the awareness and training of observers. This is not true of earthquake magnitude, which is defined by objective measurements such as the amplitude of the maximum shaking shown in a seismogram and the length of a fault rupture. Unlike intensity, magnitude is defined by science to be independent of the distance of the observer from the epicentre. It is, so to speak, the amount of explosive in a bomb, as opposed to the bomb's effects, that is, the intensity of an explosion. Another comparison, favoured by Richter, is that magnitude is like the power output of a radio station (measured in kilowatts) while intensity is like the signal strength of the station, which depends on the listener's location and the radio waves' propagation path from the station to the listener. An earthquake can have only one magnitude, fundamentally; but it will have many intensities.

That said, magnitude is a more difficult concept than intensity for the public to understand. It is also measured in many

Seismologist Charles
Richter (1900–1985),
c. 1925.

more ways than the initial scale devised by Richter in the 1930s. 'The concept of magnitude is a good example of the inability of the vast majority of seismologists to communicate adequately with the general public', complains Philip Fradkin, a Pulitzer Prize-winning journalist formerly at the *Los Angeles Times*, in his book on 'earthquakes and life along the San Andreas fault'.[3] He therefore decided to avoid any reference to magnitude in the book, so far as he could. Nevertheless, the title of his book – perhaps chosen by his publisher – is *Magnitude 8*. No newspaper report on an earthquake – whether in California or any other place – is considered complete without a statement of its magnitude.

To understand magnitude, we have first to understand more about earthquake waves. There are two basic types of earthquake wave, as Michell first perceived after the Lisbon earthquake: *body* waves, which propagate from the earthquake's focus underground (the so-called hypocentre) to the point on the surface directly above the hypocentre (the epicentre); and *surface* waves, which are produced by the transformation of some body waves on reaching the surface. The body waves consist of primary (P) waves, and secondary (S) waves. Two important types of surface wave – the Love wave and the Rayleigh wave – were named after the mathematician A.E.H. Love and the physicist John William Strutt, Lord Rayleigh, who defined them in 1911 and 1885 respectively.

P waves travel fastest, up to 6.5 kilometres (4 miles) per second; a P wave travels from Alaska to Hawaii in about seven minutes, whereas a tsunami takes five hours. The first movement felt in an earthquake is therefore caused by a P wave. It moves fastest because it is condensational, like a sound wave, compressing and expanding rock and liquid in the same direction in which it moves. On reaching the surface, it makes the ground – and a seismograph – move principally along the vertical axis. The initial movement can either be upwards or downwards, depending on the direction of the fault movement at the hypocentre. The P wave also compresses the air at the surface, sometimes creating the 'express-train' roar of a big earthquake.

Body waves and
surface waves
produced by
earthquakes.

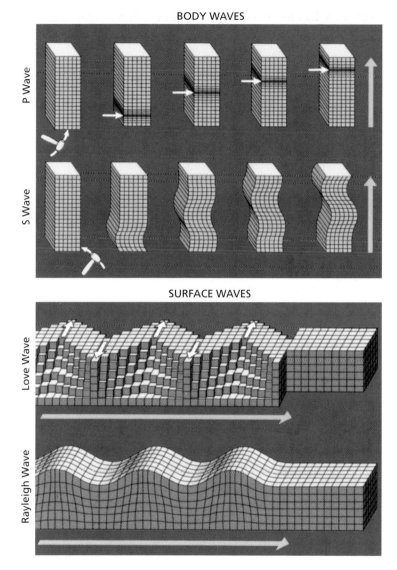

The S wave, by contrast, is distortional: it moves with a side-to-side shearing motion, like a radio wave, and this makes it slower and unable to travel through liquids (hence the fact that ships at sea detect P waves from an earthquake, but not S waves). It makes the ground move both vertically and horizontally. Since buildings can stand but little horizontal stress, S waves do far more damage

99

than P waves. If we recall the description of the beginning of the Great Kanto earthquake by the seismologist Imamura, it was the P waves that Imamura reported as arriving first, but it was the slightly later S waves that damaged his laboratory at the Tokyo Imperial University. In many earthquakes mine workers experience less shaking than people above ground, because those underground are shaken only by P waves and not by S waves.

The difference in the arrival times of P and S waves from a given earthquake, as determined by a seismograph, can be used to calculate the location of its epicentre. In principle, the method requires seismograms of the earthquake from three or more seismographs in different locations – preferably distributed reasonably uniformly around the epicentre – so as to 'triangulate' the epicentre. However, the process is not straightforward. In practice dozens of reports from seismographic stations may be used to pin down an epicentre, along with considerable computing power. The International Seismological Centre in the United Kingdom, which originally grew from the worldwide monitoring of earthquakes by John Milne at his home on the Isle of Wight in the early twentieth century, uses the readings from 60 or more seismographic stations around the world to locate, for example, the epicentre of a moderate-sized earthquake at the Mid-Atlantic Ridge under the Atlantic Ocean.

At its simplest the method relies on the fact that the further away an earthquake epicentre is from a seismograph, the larger will be the difference in arrival time between the faster P waves and the slower S waves. The precise difference in arrival time will depend on the type of rock(s) through which the waves travel. Yet seismologists can employ average differences in arrival time based on data from thousands of previous earthquakes in order to calculate epicentres. They have compiled tables and graphs showing the average arrival time of P and S waves for any specified distance from a seismograph. By comparing the P and S arrival times for a new earthquake with the average time in the table or graph, they can read off the distance between the seismograph and the epicentre (strictly speaking, the hypocentre) of the earthquake.

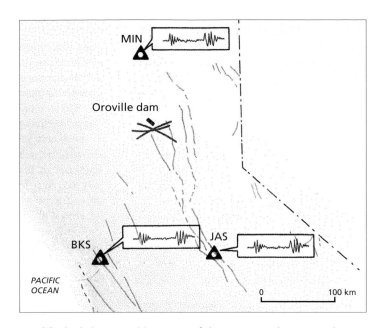

To find the actual location of the epicentre by triangulation,
they take the estimated distances from the earthquake of three
seismographs and, figuratively speaking, draw three circles with
their centres at the locations of the three seismographs and their
radii equal to the three estimated distances. (The calculation is
nowadays done by computer.) The point where the three circles
intersect – or, in practice, the area enclosed by the arcs of the
three circles – is the location of the epicentre.

Bruce Bolt, former director of the seismographic stations at
the University of California at Berkeley, gives a real example in
his book *Earthquakes and Geological Discovery*. On 1 August 1975
an earthquake of magnitude 5.7 was recorded in northeastern
California. Its P waves arrived at the Berkeley seismographic
station (BKS) at 15.46 hours and 4.5 seconds; its S waves at 15.46
hours and 25.5 seconds. Thus the difference in time (S minus P)
was 21.0 seconds, giving an estimated distance of 190 kilometres
(118 miles). The difference in S and P wave times for two other
Californian stations was 20.4 seconds (for Jamestown, JAS) and
12.9 seconds (for Mineral, MIN), giving estimated distances of
188 kilometres and 105 kilometres respectively. The arcs of three

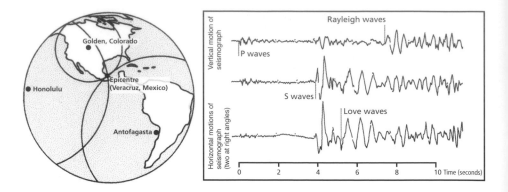

circles centred at Berkeley (radius 190 kilometres), Jamestown (radius 188 kilometres) and Mineral (105 kilometres), intersected approximately near the town of Oroville, giving an estimated epicentre of 39.5°N 121.5°W, with an uncertainty of about 10 kilometres. (The depth of the hypocentre was unknown, and would have required more data to calculate it.)

Another example of the calculation of an epicentre given by Bolt – this time international – is provided by a magnitude-5.5 earthquake with its epicentre near Veracruz, Mexico, on 11 March 1967. Here the seismographic stations selected are at Antofagasta (Chile), Honolulu (Hawaii) and Golden (Colorado). The seismogram shows three traces made by the US Geological Survey at Golden. The top trace shows the vertical motion of the seismograph; the middle and bottom traces show the horizontal motions (at right angles to each other). The P waves arrive first, followed four seconds later by the first of the S waves; then the Love and Rayleigh waves arrive. By combining the information from several seismograms of this earthquake obtained at various stations, in addition to Antofagasta, Honolulu and Golden, scientists calculated the epicentre to lie at 19.10°N 95.80°W, in the sea just east of Veracruz, and the hypocentre to be 33 kilometres (20.5 miles) down. There were three injuries and moderate property damage at Veracruz.

The greater the number of stations that provide P and S wave data for an earthquake, the better. In the words of Bolt:

Calculation of the epicentre of an earthquake in Mexico, 1967.

More precise locations and wave measurements of distant earthquakes can be obtained using linked seismographic stations. Such links may be either by electrical wire connections or, for arrays with large distances between seismographs, by having accurate clocks or radio receivers [notably the Global Positioning System, or GPS] place universal time marks at intervals on each record. It is this common time-base that turns a group of recorders in a region into a seismic array. The great advantage for earthquake analysis is that seismic wave variations from neighbouring stations across the array can be correlated with high precision. The gradients of such variations can be directly related by theoretical formula to the propagation paths of the waves.[4]

The first linked international networks of stations date from the mid-1960s, during the Cold War, when they were set up to monitor underground nuclear tests after the Partial Test Ban Treaty of 1963 which restricted nuclear testing to underground sites. For instance, the defence department of the US government established the World Wide Standardized Seismographic Network, which was virtually complete by 1967. However, seismographic networks turned out to be good at measuring the locations and magnitudes of large nuclear explosions, but not so good at distinguishing small nuclear tests from natural seismicity, although seismologists were helped by the fact that military bureaucracies tend to schedule bomb tests exactly on the hour.

To come now to the measurement of magnitude – a more complicated concept than epicentre and intensity – the problem faced by twentieth-century seismologists wishing to determine the size of an earthquake was how to devise a scale that would allot a single number to each earthquake, rather than the many numbers of an intensity scale, which vary according to the distance of the observer from the epicentre. With just a single number per earthquake, the size of different earthquakes might then be compared.

In 1932 Richter devised an empirical formula to do this for moderate earthquakes in southern California, when measured by a particular kind of seismograph used at his institution, Caltech: the Wood-Anderson seismograph. This had been invented in 1925 by two American seismologists. Richter's formula related the distance of the seismograph from the epicentre (measured in kilometres), as derived from the difference in S and P wave arrival times, to the maximum amplitude of ground motion shown in the seismogram, as shown by the maximum height of the S waves (measured in thousandths of a millimetre). The larger the distance from the epicentre, of course, the smaller the maximum amplitude. For moderate earthquakes in southern California, the distance from the epicentre and the maximum amplitude of the shaking are found to be inversely proportional.

Because earthquakes vary in size over a huge range, Richter chose to compress the maximum amplitude by expressing it as a logarithm to the base 10. Thus an amplitude of 10 thousandths

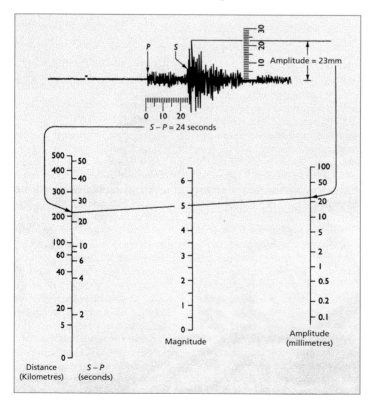

How to calculate the Richter magnitude of an earthquake – in this case, magnitude 5.

of a millimetre was given a logarithmic value of 1; of 100 thousandths of a millimetre, a value of 2; of 1,000 thousandths of a millimetre (that is, 1 millimetre), a value of 3; and of 10,000 thousandths of a millimetre (that is, 10 millimetres or 1 centimetre), a value of 4; and so on for earthquakes of greater size. Richter also selected a standard distance from the epicentre of 100 kilometres. Then, according to his definition, an earthquake 100 kilometres away from a Wood-Anderson seismograph that shows a maximum wave amplitude of 10 millimetres has a magnitude of 4. If instead the seismograph is 200 kilometres away, with the same maximum wave amplitude the magnitude rises to about 4.5, or if the seismograph is only 20 kilometres away, the magnitude falls to about 2.7. If, on the other hand, the seismograph remains 100 kilometres away from the earthquake but records a maximum wave amplitude of 100 millimetres (100,000 thousandths of a millimetre) – 10 times the previous maximum amplitude – then the magnitude is 5. In other words, the Richter scale is not linear. Increase the magnitude of an earthquake by 1, and you get a *10*-fold increase in amplitude of shaking. An earthquake of magnitude 8 shakes the ground 10 times more than one of magnitude 7, and 100 times more than one of magnitude 6. Nevertheless, a magnitude-6 earthquake may be more destructive than a magnitude-8 earthquake if its epicentre happens to coincide with a heavily populated area.

The physical meaning of the Richter magnitude scale is not easy to grasp. In fact, a leading American nature writer, John McPhee, remarked that he had 'no idea how the scale works' in his book *Assembling California*. 'Richter was a professor at Caltech. His scale . . . is understood by professors at Caltech and a percentage of the rest of the population too small to be expressed as a number.'[5] Richter himself admitted that it was 'a rather rough and ready procedure . . . The most remarkable feature about the magnitude scale was that it worked at all.'[6]

The Richter scale was somewhat controversial from the beginning of its adoption. When it first appeared in print in 1935 in the leading US seismological journal, Richter was credited as sole author of the scale. As with many breakthroughs, its paternity was soon disputed. At the time of its invention, Richter was working closely with his distinguished colleague Gutenberg (Einstein's friend), who suggested that the scale should be logarithmic. A second Caltech colleague, Harry Wood, one of the two inventors of the Wood-Anderson seismograph, proposed 'magnitude' as the correct term to distinguish the concept from 'intensity' – himself borrowing the idea from the stellar magnitude scale used by astronomers to describe the brightness of stars. Moreover, an earlier paper, published in 1931 by the Japanese seismologist Kiyoo Wadati, had indicated how to allow for the distance of a seismograph from the epicentre, although Wadati had not gone on from this to produce any magnitude scale.

Richter freely acknowledged these American and Japanese contributions in print, but even so he 'felt a unique sense of ownership about his scale', writes the geophysicist Susan Hough in her biography of Richter, given his undoubtedly enormous investment of effort in measuring earthquakes and calculating their magnitudes.[7] Hough supports Richter's claim to sole authorship of the magnitude scale, but discusses fully and fairly the views of many seismologists that the correct name should be the 'Gutenberg-Richter scale'. The issue remains sensitive, with the *Encyclopaedia Britannica* attributing the 'Richter' scale to both Gutenberg and Richter.

More importantly, Richter's original scale was never universally applicable to earthquakes of all sizes and in all locations around the world. For a start it was based on a specific design of seismograph, operating in the particular seismic conditions prevalent in southern California. The Wood-Anderson instrument has now been superseded by seismographs that can respond to the very lowest wave frequencies generated by earthquakes, which are a particular feature of the largest events. Second, it works properly only for earthquakes with magnitudes no greater than approximately 5.5; above this figure, calculated Richter magnitudes 'saturate', meaning that they fail to increase proportionately with increase in earthquake size. Finally, Richter magnitude – being based simply on the maximum recorded amplitude of S waves –

cannot distinguish between two earthquakes that generate the same peak amplitude but over a shorter and a longer duration.

That said, despite their increasing sophistication, other magnitude scales in use have their limitations, too, whereas 'every magnitude scale used today can trace its lineage directly to Charles Richter's scale', says Hough.[8] It would have been better, in her view, to have adopted the 'Modified Richter Scale' as an umbrella term – as was done when the original 1902 Mercalli scale of intensity was modified in 1931. Instead, after half a century of dominance 'Richter magnitude' has nowadays been generally replaced by simply 'magnitude', not only in scientific journals but also in the reporting of earthquakes in the news.

The dominant magnitude scale today is technically known as a 'moment magnitude' scale and, like Richter's scale, it is logarithmic, not linear. *Seismic moment*, though hard to define without mathematics, is a physical quantity related to the total energy released in an earthquake, which can be converted into a moment magnitude. The energy released by a moment magnitude-6 earthquake is about 32 times more than that released by one of moment magnitude 5, and is almost 1,000 (about 32^2) times more energetic than an earthquake of moment magnitude 4. The most powerful earthquake ever recorded, which happened in Chile in 1960 with a moment magnitude of 9.5, is estimated to have released fully one-quarter of the entire seismic energy release of the planet since the beginning of the twentieth century (including the great Indian Ocean earthquake of 2004) – more than 20,000 times the energy released by the atomic bomb dropped on Hiroshima in 1945. Rupturing 1,000 kilometres of fault running down Chile's coastline, the 1960 earthquake was so powerful that 'it wobbled the planet' and set seismologists, such as Caltech's Hiroo Kanamori, thinking about how to devise the new moment magnitude scale.[9]

The major benefit of seismic moment and moment magnitude over Richter magnitude is that they can be estimated both by the field geologists who examine the geometry of a fault and by the seismologists who analyse seismograms. Moment is defined in terms of fault rigidity multiplied by fault area multiplied by slip distance, all of which can in principle be measured. None of these, of course, appears in Richter's formula, which involves only the distance from the epicentre to the seismograph and the seismogram's maximum amplitude, and which has nothing to say about fault structure. The seismologist Seth Stein explains:

> We have a good idea of the fault's rigidity, or strength, from both earthquake studies and lab experiments on rocks. The area of the fault can be estimated from seismograms. Another way is to look at the locations of aftershocks, which are smaller earthquakes that happen after a big earthquake. Because these are on and near the fault plane, the aftershocks map out the area of the fault that moved. Dividing the measured seismic moment by the rigidity and fault area shows how far the fault slipped. If the earthquake ruptured the earth's surface, these values can be checked by measuring the length of surface rupture and the amount of offset across it.[10]

Although moment magnitude approximately matches past magnitude scales, its introduction has meant the downgrading of some historic earthquakes; for example, the San Francisco earthquake of 1906, once estimated to be of magnitude 8.3, is now reckoned at about 7.8. It is unwise to put too much faith in any single magnitude scale, warns Stein. After the Indian Ocean quake in 2004, he and a colleague, Emile Okal, upgraded the earthquake from a magnitude of 9.0 to 9.3. This gained them worldwide media attention. But, Stein says, 'the number itself was not important. The important fact was that the area that had slipped was three times bigger than first thought.' An area of staggering dimensions near Sumatra, about 1,200 kilometres (750 miles) long and 200 kilometres wide – similar in size to the whole of California – was found to have slipped about 10 metres (33 feet). 'Because that part of the fault had just slipped, it would be hundreds of years before it could generate another huge tsunami like the one that had just killed more than 200,000 people.'[11]

Such figures do more to make the incredible power of great earthquakes real to the public than a logarithmic magnitude figure in the range up to a maximum of 10, however valuable magnitude figures may be to scientists. Some seismologists have therefore tried to create linear magnitude scales that are more approachable for non-specialists. One such example was published in 1990, after the Loma Prieta earthquake in California in 1989, by Arch Johnston, an American seismologist working in the seismically less active middle of the United States. Johnson has a particular interest in publicizing his discipline, and confesses:

> Let's face it: seismologists do a pretty poor job of communicating the facts about our science to the public. Earthquake magnitude is the classic example. How many of us have struggled to explain the Richter scale? We explain that it is logarithmic, with each unit indicating a factor of 10 increase, but this really represents a factor of 32 increase in intrinsic earthquake size, and in any case we don't use the Richter scale anymore. By then the unfortunate listener is reeling and can be dispatched quietly by mentioning negative magnitudes or saturation. We even wonder why the audience or the reporter has this glazed look when we finish.[12]

Energy release of earthquakes compared with other natural and man-made explosions.

Instead of the standard earthquake magnitude scale, Johnston's so-called Earthquake Strength Scale allots a strength of 1 to a

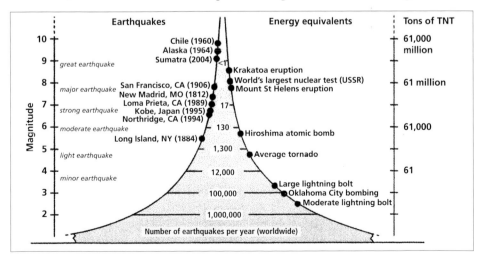

magnitude-5.0 earthquake, that is, at the threshold of damage; a strength of 100 to the magnitude-7.0 Loma Prieta earthquake in the San Francisco Bay Area in 1989; a strength of 10,000 to the magnitude-9.2 Alaska earthquake of 1964; and a strength of 31,600 to the biggest earthquake of all, the magnitude-9.5 event in Chile in 1960. Johnston's scale also compares the energy released from earthquakes to that released by other kinds of natural disaster. His suggested moment magnitude for a tornado is 4.7; for the Mount St Helens volcanic eruption of 1980, 7.8; and for a well-developed hurricane over a ten-day lifespan, a mighty moment magnitude of 9.6.

6 Faults, Plates and Drifting Continents

While the measurement of earthquakes made steady progress during the past century or so, the growth in the theoretical understanding of earthquake mechanisms was less impressive. The plate tectonic theory invented in the 1960s may have triumphantly explained most – though certainly not all – of the macroscopic incidence of earthquakes, as we shall see. Yet the microscopic picture – in other words, what happens to the rocks underground during an earthquake – remains to a great extent the model proposed a century ago after the great San Francisco earthquake of 1906, with all its faults, in both the normal and the geological sense of that word.

It was in the first decade of the twentieth century that the tectonic movement of geological faults came to be seen as the chief origin of earthquakes. Until then volcanic action had been considered a strong contender as a cause of earthquakes, partly because much of the early research on seismology emerged from southern Italy, a land with long experience of both destructive earthquakes, for example those in Calabria in 1783 and near Naples in 1857, and contiguous active volcanoes, such as Mount Vesuvius and Mount Etna. Subsequently, however, careful studies of volcanoes demonstrated that volcanic activity was often free from earthquakes, and that earthquakes frequently occurred far from volcanoes.

The seismologist John Milne was an assiduous climber of Japanese volcanoes from the 1870s onwards. In 1877 he and others chartered a special steamer to visit the erupting volcano of

Surface rupture/
fissure, Olema,
California, after the
great San Francisco
earthquake of 1906.

Oshima, a small island in Sagami Bay to the south of Yokohama. Milne reported from the island that 'Earthquakes, although so common on the mainland, are said not to occur here and the only shocks that have been felt are those which were produced at the time of the breaking out of the volcano.'[1] Much later, he concluded:

> In Japan, the majority of earthquakes which we experience do *not* come from volcanoes nor do they seem to have any direct connection with them. In the centre of Japan there are mountainous districts where active volcanoes are numerous, yet the area is singularly free from earthquakes.[2]

By 1905 Milne's colleague Charles Davison (the expert on British earthquakes) could write: 'That tectonic earthquakes are closely connected with the formation of faults seems now established beyond doubt. They occur far from all traces of recent volcanic action.'[3]

In 1906 the San Francisco earthquake produced a huge surface rupture measuring 435 kilometres (270 miles). To explain how this had occurred, the American geophysicist Harry Fielding Reid came up with his mechanism of 'elastic rebound'. This theory begins with the idea of a fault as a joint between two rock planes. The joint is usually not exactly vertical and so one plane of the fault overhangs the other. If the overhanging plane moves downwards, the fault is termed 'normal'; if it moves upwards, it is termed a 'reverse' fault. Movement in the vertical axis is known as 'dip-slip', that in the horizontal axis as 'strike-slip'. Of course, a real fault often shows both kinds of slip. Friction between the two planes of the fault controls its movement or lack of movement. The lower the friction, the weaker the fault and the more easily it slips. If the friction is low enough, the fault may slip constantly and aseismically; this is known as 'fault creep'. If it is of medium size the fault may slip frequently, producing many small earthquakes. But if the friction is high the fault may slip only occasionally, and there will be few, but large, earthquakes.

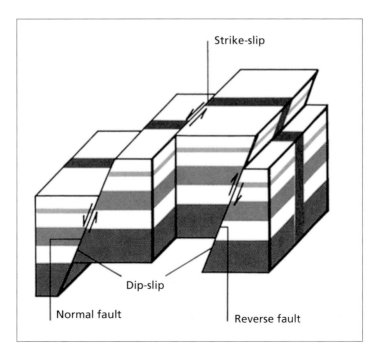

Types of geological fault.

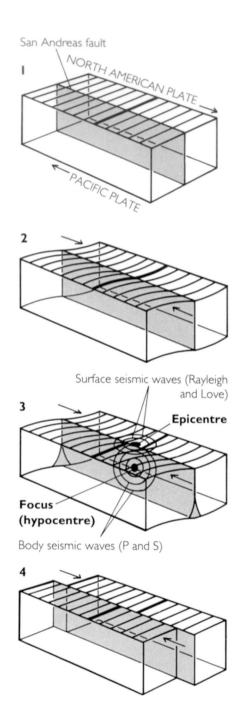

San Andreas fault

1

NORTH AMERICAN PLATE

PACIFIC PLATE

2

Surface seismic waves (Rayleigh and Love)

3

Epicentre

Focus (hypocentre)

Body seismic waves (P and S)

4

Elastic rebound model of geological fault rupture and earthquakes on the San Andreas fault, California.

Even then, the rupture may not be entirely visible at the surface, unlike that of the 1906 San Francisco earthquake.

Reid had noticed how, in the years before the earthquake, roads, fences and streams crossing the fault area had been deformed, and how after the earthquake they were displaced or offset – by up to 6.4 metres (21 feet). He proposed that before the earthquake, friction between the two sides of the fault had locked part of the fault together, deforming it as the sides moved past each other. Finally the fault snapped; the sides sprang away from each other and then elastically rebounded into less strained conformations, creating in the process the surface rupture and offsets. Although in practice this model of earthquake mechanism has many difficulties, it is still the one that is most widely employed.

The fault in question in 1906 was, of course, the now famous San Andreas fault. It was 'discovered', so to speak, by geologists investigating the San Francisco earthquake (notably Andrew Lawson), and is undoubtedly now 'the most well-known plate tectonic boundary in the world' – to quote the title of the US Geological Survey's special report on it, published in the year after the Loma Prieta earthquake of 1989. The San Andreas fault system is a great scar running up most of California, geologically highly complex, where the Pacific plate edges past the continental North American plate at the rate of 2.5–4 centimetres (1–1.5 inches) per year. Altogether, with its many adjacent faults, the system is 95 kilometres (60 miles) wide and 1,300 kilometres (800 miles) long.

Back in 1906 no geologist would have credited such a theory of movement in the earth's crust, implying, as it does, that continents move. Indeed, no one could imagine any plausible overarching explanation for the horizontal movement of faults. During the nineteenth century it was the *vertical* movement of continents that had become orthodox geology, as expressed in the works of Charles Lyell, which deeply influenced Charles Darwin in the 1830s. By the end of the century the lighter crust of the earth was thought to float buoyantly on the denser, less rigid mantle – thereby generating mountains as the crust rose and ocean basins as it sank. By contrast, the horizontal displacement

Meteorologist and geologist Alfred Wegener (1880–1930), who proposed the theory of continental drift.

of the crust – and that over thousands of kilometres – was calculated to be physically impossible: where would the enormous force required come from? It was a simple matter for physicists to show that the gravitational force necessary to shift continents through the crust would be enough to stop the rotation of the planet in less than a year.

But then how to explain – without postulating earlier physical links between the continents – the remarkable geographical fit of the Atlantic coasts of South America and Africa and the discovery of unquestionably identical fossils of plants and animals on opposite sides of the Atlantic Ocean? The fit had been spotted as long ago as the late 1500s, when a Dutch mapmaker had suggested that North and South America had been torn from Europe and Africa. In 1620 the philosopher Francis Bacon (whose followers founded the Royal Society) commented on the striking match between the continents. In 1858 a French mapmaker published maps depicting continental drift. By the first part of the twentieth century the favoured explanation for the fossils was the land bridge. The species in question had supposedly migrated over a land bridge between, say, Brazil and Africa; subsequently the bridge had been buried as the earth's crust collapsed inwards with the cooling and shrinking of the planet. (Before radioactivity was accepted as a source of heat within the earth, the consensus was that the earth was gradually cooling, losing its heat to space.)

In 1911, while pondering this unlikely theory of land bridges together with the apparent fit of Africa and South America, a versatile German meteorologist and astronomer, Alfred Wegener, became convinced that continental drift had occurred. A mega-continent which Wegener dubbed Pangaea ('all land') had broken apart and after millions of years the bits had drifted into the present continental configuration. Announcing the idea in early 1912, Wegener eventually published it as a book in Germany in 1915. A decade later it appeared in English as *The Origin of Continents and Oceans*. Before Wegener's premature death, on an expedition to Greenland in 1930, the book went through four editions and was translated into French, Swedish, Spanish and Russian.

Unfortunately for Wegener, although his radical idea – that continents move – was basically correct, his proposed mechanism and his calculations of the rate of movement were flawed. Moving continents were therefore rejected by a large majority of scientists. The typical response was that of an American geologist at the University of Chicago, Rollin Chamberlin, who said in 1928: 'If we are to believe Wegener's hypothesis we must forget everything that has been learned in the last 70 years and start all over again.'[4]

Then, in the 1960s, a mass of evidence in favour of Wegener's hypothesis – emerging from an unimpeachable diversity of scientific studies – became so overwhelming that a revolution in the earth sciences occurred. Out of the half-satisfactory notion of continental drift quickly evolved the more compelling and rigorous theory of plate tectonics. The seismologist Susan Hough compares its importance in geology to that of the circulation of blood in medicine in 'trying to fathom heart attacks'.[5] The acceptance of plate tectonics by geologists was certainly a lot speedier than that of blood circulation by physicians. 'Within a few years, from about 1963 to 1970, continental drift went from a strange idea to accepted. It became the core of plate tectonics, the most

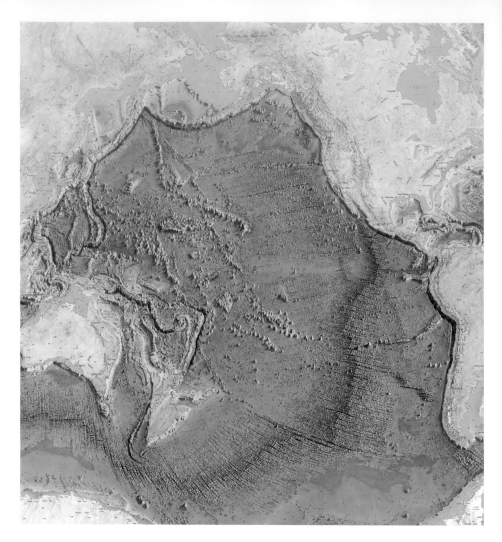

important concept in geology', wrote the seismologist Seth Stein in 2010.[6] Stein trained in geophysics at the California Institute of Technology in the mid-1970s, where he was in the first generation of geologists to learn plate tectonics in graduate classes.

The earliest – and probably the most compelling – pieces of evidence for the new theory involved earthquakes. The data came from the floor of the Atlantic Ocean. The existence of a mountain range beneath the mid-Atlantic had been suspected since the 1850s. In 1947 scientists from the Woods Hole Oceanographic Institution in Massachusetts began to plot the shape of this

Map of the floors of the oceans by Bruce Heezen and Marie Tharp, 1977.

Mid-Atlantic Ridge using the most powerful depth sounders then available. The ridge was found to run down the centre of the Atlantic, roughly equidistant from the continental coasts on either side. It boasted peaks up to 3,000 metres (10,000 feet) high, a mile below the surface of the ocean. Dredge samples revealed that the rocks of the ridge were of volcanic origin and much younger than they had expected; there was far less sediment on the ocean floor than predicted on the basis of ocean floors having been formed early in the history of the earth. Bruce Heezen, a geologist involved in the research, became so fascinated that he and Marie Tharp, his drafting assistant, began to collect depth recordings from all over the world and from them to create the first profiles and maps of the ocean floors. It was one of these maps that led to a breakthrough. The Mid-Atlantic Ridge showed a deep V-shaped valley running along the centre of its entire length. When Heezen took this map and plotted on it the epicentres of Atlantic earthquakes that were then being studied by other scientists, he suddenly realized that the earthquakes were taking place in the rift valley of the ridge. A parallel plot of breaks in transatlantic cables coincided with the earthquake data: the cables broke over the rift valley.

This was in around 1956. Between then and 1960 American and British oceanographic expeditions trailed the world's oceans with depth recorders, tracing their ridge systems. These were found to run along the centre of the Indian Ocean as well as the centre of the Atlantic; to link together south of Africa; and to connect with a ridge midway between Australia and Antarctica that linked to a ridge that ran northwards through the eastern Pacific (the East Pacific Rise) until it reached California. A rift valley was not always found at the centre of a ridge; often whole ridge segments were offset from each other by as much as several hundred kilometres along tremendous fractures in the oceanic crust, which were sites of earthquakes. Measurements of the heat flow along the crest of the Mid-Atlantic Ridge gave a figure up to eight times greater than elsewhere on the ocean floor. Clearly, the surface of the earth beneath the oceans had once been – and probably was still being – torn apart and remoulded on a grand scale.

In 1960 Harry Hess, another American geologist, came up with a fundamentally new explanation of these observations couched in suitably cautious language, mindful as he was of the hostility of his colleagues towards Wegener's ideas. 'The birth of the oceans is a matter of conjecture, the subsequent history is obscure, and the present structure is just beginning to be understood', Hess began. His paper on the subject, he warned readers, was 'an essay in geopoetry'.[7] Rather than the drifting continents favoured by Wegener, Hess focused on the ocean floors. The floors behaved like twin conveyor belts carrying the continents, he suggested; molten new crust welled up at ridges/rifts and moved away from the ridge on either side in opposite directions, while old crust was simultaneously destroyed in the deep ocean trenches that lie near the edges of the continents. This 'sea-floor spreading' (the name soon given to the theory by the geologist Robert Dietz) was calculated by Hess to proceed at the rate of about 1.25 centimetres (half an inch) a year on each side of the ridge. At this pace the spreading should have created the ocean floors of the world in just 200 million years, rather than the 1 or 2 billion years formerly imagined – an age that agreed with the measured age of the oldest rocks discovered there.

Not until the 1970s were scientists able to obtain eyewitness evidence of volcanic activity at ocean rifts, when submersibles examined recent formations of lava at the Mid-Atlantic Ridge at close range. (They could, however, watch the fiery birth of Surtsey, a new volcanic island that in 1963 suddenly rose from the sea south of Iceland above the ridge.) But in the meantime they conceived an ingenious new way of extracting new evidence for the theory of sea-floor spreading. Samples of rock taken from ocean ridges showed a curious pattern of magnetism. Those from the East Pacific Rise south of Easter Island were particularly remarkable: the magnetism in the rocks, with an impressive symmetry about the axis of the ridge, switched back and forth in direction,

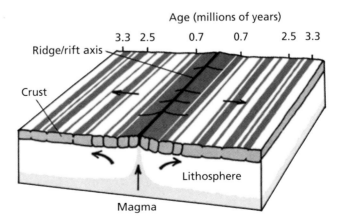

Sea-floor spreading. The measurement of these magnetic 'zebra' patterns in ocean floor rocks was an important clue to the existence of tectonic plates and their direction of movement.

Age (millions of years)

3.3 2.5   0.7   0.7   2.5 3.3

Ridge/rift axis

Crust

Lithosphere

Magma

making a 'zebra' pattern: black stripes indicated magnetization in one direction and the intervening white gaps indicated magnetization in the reverse direction.

These patterns proved to be 'the true Rosetta Stone of plate tectonics', writes Hough – 'the key that won over a sceptical community'.[8] Two British oceanographers, Frederick Vine and Drummond Matthews, were the first to explain the magnetic geological phenomenon in a paper written in 1963. From other scientific studies they knew that the earth's magnetic field had reversed direction frequently in its history – the north magnetic pole becoming the south magnetic pole and vice versa. The geological record showed that the switch had occurred at least three or four times every million years during the past 70 million years. They therefore proposed that when the molten rock (magma) extruded at an ocean ridge had cooled down, it retained its original direction of magnetism when the earth's magnetic field subsequently reversed. New volcanic rock, by contrast, forcing apart the cooled volcanic rock, became magnetized in the reverse direction. The bands of magnetism stretching away symmetrically on either side of an ocean ridge were therefore a fossil record of the earth's magnetism over the period that rock was extruded at the ridge. 'The crust can thus be viewed as a twin-headed tape recorder in which the reversal history of the earth's magnetic field is registered', Vine wrote in 1990.[9] And since the dating of the pole reversals was available independently, the rate of sea-floor spreading, too, could be calculated from these measurements.

The scene was now set for the development of plate tectonics. In 1965 the Canadian geophysicist John Tuzo Wilson suggested that, rather than Wegener's hypothesis of rigid continents somehow drifting through a malleable crust, the earth's crust was composed of 'several large rigid plates' that were growing at some edges and being destroyed at others, and that were also moving across the earth.[10] 'Tectonics' – from the Greek *tekton*, meaning 'builder' – was added in 1968–9 by others; the word had long been used by geologists to describe dynamic processes such as mountain building, as in the earlier quoted 'tectonic earthquake' remark by Davison. A plate, wrote Wilson, had three kinds of boundary with other plates:

ocean ridges/rifts, where two plates grew; ocean trenches, where a plate was destroyed by sinking beneath a second plate; and what he termed 'transform faults', where colliding plates were neither enlarged nor diminished. The San Andreas fault of California was a transform fault, he proposed.

Wilson's basic picture of tectonic plates still stands. Today scientists count seven major plates, often known as the Pacific, Indo-Australian, Eurasian, African, North American, South American and Antarctic plates. There are also many minor ones, such as the Arabian plate, the precise number and shape of which are disputed. The average plate thickness is nearly 100 kilometres (60 miles). More than 90 per cent of known plate tectonic boundaries lie underwater; only rarely do they pop up above ground, as in the San Andreas fault, the North Anatolian fault in Turkey and numerous faults in central China.

Most of the world's earthquakes occur at plate boundaries. The plotting of epicentres of quakes on a map of the world – first undertaken by Mallet in the 1850s – shows that 999 out of 1,000 earthquakes, and an even larger fraction of those of high magnitude, occur in certain belts, which generally correspond with plate boundaries. (There is an element of circularity here, though, because the location of earthquakes is one of the pieces of information used by geologists to work out where the boundaries are.) A map of earthquake hypocentres is revealing, too. As discovered by Wadati in the 1920s, the hypocentres of earthquakes near Pacific Ocean trenches such as the Tonga Trench and the Japan Trench are all shallow, within the top 16 kilometres (10 miles) of the earth's crust. But as earthquakes move westwards towards Asia, away from the Japan Trench, their hypocentres deepen dramatically: they are 80 to 160 kilometres (50 to 150 miles) below the Japanese islands, 480 kilometres under the Sea of Japan, and 640 kilometres beneath the coast of Manchuria. This, too, is to be expected at many plate boundaries, for the following reason.

Recall that at the boundaries friction and stress occur, and rock is either extruded from the mantle in molten form (at ridges) or melted anew by being forced back into the mantle (at trenches)

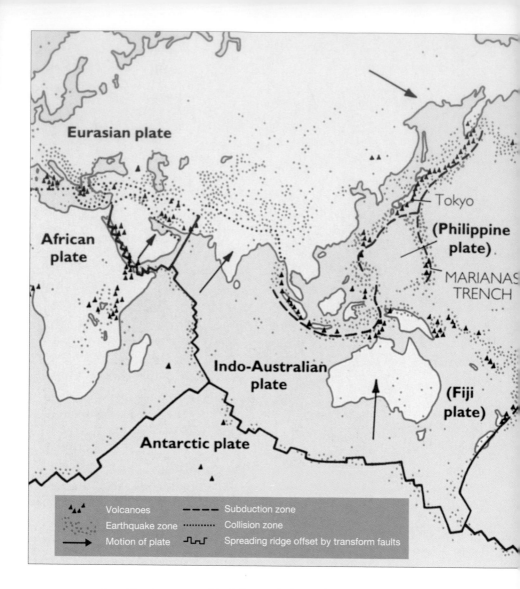

Eurasian plate

African plate

Tokyo

(Philippine plate)

MARIANAS TRENCH

Indo-Australian plate

(Fiji plate)

Antarctic plate

▲▲▲	Volcanoes	– – – –	Subduction zone
⣿⣿	Earthquake zone	··········	Collision zone
⟶	Motion of plate	⌐_⌐_	Spreading ridge offset by transform faults

– a process of swallowing termed 'subduction'. As a plate dives into the depths of the earth, part of it, as it melts, is thought to find its way back to the surface in the form of volcanoes; the details of the process are largely unknown.

Subduction was responsible for the greatest earthquakes of the past century, those in Chile in 1960, Alaska in 1964 and Indonesia in 2004. In Chile the subduction of the Pacific plate beneath the South American plate is currently occurring at the

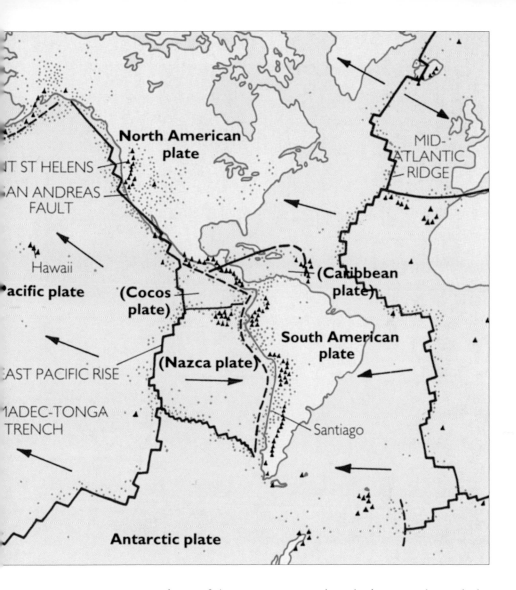

MT ST HELENS

SAN ANDREAS
FAULT

Hawaii

Pacific plate

EAST PACIFIC RISE

KADEC-TONGA
TRENCH

North American
plate

MID-
ATLANTIC
RIDGE

(Cocos
plate)

(Caribbean
plate)

(Nazca plate)

South American
plate

Santiago

Antarctic plate

Map showing
the tectonic plates
of the world and
their directions
of movement.

rapid rate of about 8 centimetres (3 inches) per year beneath the
Andes mountain range, which is growing in height as a consequence. It is also occurring beneath the island arcs of Japan and
Tonga, where the Pacific plate dips down beneath the Eurasian
plate at an angle of 35 degrees and more in an extensive subduction zone, thereby creating earthquakes with hypocentres at
increasing depth the deeper the plate goes. On the northwest
Pacific coast of the United States it is believed that subduction

Mount St Helens, Washington, before and after its eruption, 1980.

is taking place beyond the northern end of the San Andreas fault, where a subducted plate is thought to have disappeared beneath the North American plate in recent geological time, leaving the majestic volcanoes of the Cascades range as evidence of its past existence. (One of these, Mount St Helens, erupted spectacularly in 1980.) Today, however, the Pacific plate is not being subducted beneath the North American plate, but instead is grinding past it. The hypocentres of Californian earthquakes are therefore shallow, like those at or near Pacific ocean trenches; the rock deep beneath California is comparatively undisturbed.

In fact, subduction may occur at any plate boundary where two plates of sufficiently different density collide. In such cases the denser plate is subducted beneath the less dense plate. If, by contrast, the two colliding plates are of similar density, there will be no subduction; mountain ranges and earthquakes will still result, but generally there will be no volcanoes. This is the case in the Himalayas, where the plate on which India is located is piling into the plate on which the rest of Asia rides. Here there are frequent earthquakes, such as those in northern Afghanistan and Kashmir (the Hindu Kush), but no known volcanoes.

The explanations of earthquakes generated by plate tectonics have a 'seductive elegance', in the words of one geophysicist. In the science-fiction novel *Richter 10*, written by Arthur C. Clarke and Mike McQuay in 1996, an expert even puts forward a plan to stop earthquakes forever by 'spot welding' the tectonic plates at about 50 strategic places. The welding is to be accomplished by exploding nuclear bombs deep inside the earth, so that there is no impact on the surface.

Lava lake at the summit of Kīlauea, Hawaii.

Eruption of La Soufrière and simultaneous earthquake, Guadeloupe, 1843.

However, the explanations can conceal some awkward facts. For a start, what causes the plates to move; when did the process begin; and has it been continual or intermittent during the long history of the planet? None of the answers to these questions is at all obvious. Wegener favoured the centrifugal force generated by the spinning of the earth and the gravitational attraction of the sun and the moon as driving forces for his drifting continents. Today, geophysicists try to explain plate tectonics in terms of heat and molten rock rising upwards to the crust from the mantle and core of the earth, like a fire under a saucepan of water. A few of them propose that living organisms, by generating limestone sediments (the remains of sea creatures) on ocean floors at the margins of the continents, may eventually have altered the chemistry and temperature of the crustal rocks and induced instability, and hence plate tectonic movement. If plate tectonics really did begin with the evolution of life, then it cannot be as old as the origin of the earth, about 4.5 billion years ago. But its action is certainly responsible for producing the natural resources, such as oil and gas, required to power modern human societies.

Second, there are many aspects of present-day seismic and volcanic activity that are anomalous, according to plate tectonic theory. Consider intraplate earthquakes. Hawaii, for instance, has famous volcanoes such as Kilauea, and also experiences destructive earthquakes (nine in the past century and a half). Yet Hawaii is located near the centre of the Pacific plate, very far from the accepted plate boundaries. Consider also the Indo-Australian plate that is butting into the Eurasian plate. In addition to the earthquakes in the Himalayas – which are readily explained by plate tectonics – there have been large earthquakes in the centre of the Indo-Australian plate, which, being supposedly rigid, should be incapable of deforming in the way said to cause earthquakes. In fact, significant intraplate earthquakes have occurred in a number of locations. Within the North American plate three violent earthquakes, among the greatest known in the United States, took place in 1811–12 in Missouri; there was another large one in Charleston, South Carolina, in 1886; a magnitude-5.9 quake shook the nation's capital, Washington, DC, in 2011.

Within the Indo-Australian plate a series of magnitude-6 earthquakes ruptured the surface in Australia's Northern Territory in 1988; while in 2001 a magnitude-7.6 quake destroyed the Indian city of Bhuj in Gujarat several hundred kilometres away from the active plate boundary. Within the Eurasian plate, in western Europe, a destructive earthquake hit the Dutch/Belgian/German border in 1992, while in Britain there have been many moderately destructive earthquakes over the centuries, as we know.

The great depth of many earthquakes is also a puzzle. The subduction theory seems to offer a reasonable explanation until one learns of occasional earthquakes at depth in places where there is no apparent subduction. In 1977, for instance, Bucharest in Romania was shaken by an earthquake with a hypocentre 160 kilometres (100 miles) down in which 1,500 people died. This might be attributed to an old subduction zone obscured by later tectonic activity; not so the tremors recorded beneath Spain, north Africa and central India. Rather more seriously, physics does not in fact expect *any* earthquakes below about 50 kilometres (30 miles) – some calculations indicate a much smaller figure – because rock in a laboratory, when squeezed at analogous temperatures and pressures, becomes ductile and flows rather than fractures. Indeed, without such ductility of rocks at depth, there could be no moving tectonic plates to fracture near the surface during earthquakes.

Attempts have been made to explain all these awkward facts by postulating less rigid and uniform plates containing faults, which create intraplate earthquakes, and 'hot spots', responsible for the volcanoes of Hawaii. But scientists are obliged to recognize these exceptions as significant weaknesses in the present theory of crustal movement. 'What moves has become clearer in the twentieth century; why and when remain a mystery', remarks Philip Fradkin in his book about the San Andreas fault.[11] The theory of earthquakes rests on shakier ground than twenty-first-century seismologists would wish.

7 California: The Enigma of the San Andreas Fault

The geological origins of the San Andreas fault were brilliantly suggested in 1965 by the pioneer of plate tectonics, John Tuzo Wilson. He postulated that the fault was a transform fault between two spreading ocean ridges within the Pacific plate. Later analysis by others elaborated his idea with calculations that took account of the forces acting globally on the Pacific plate, and con - firmed the general picture of the Pacific plate slipping past – and sometimes sticking against – the North American plate, rather than being subducted as it is in the western Pacific (beneath the Eurasian plate).

The detailed picture is infinitely harder to unravel, alas, despite decades of labour and state-of-the-art instruments monitoring every conceivable aspect of the fault on and near its surface, and, from 2003 onwards, a borehole drilled into the fault's enigmatic depths (known as the San Andreas Fault Observatory at Depth, SAFOD). What has become increasingly clear is the complexity of its geology. Rather than speaking of the San Andreas fault, scientists refer now to the San Andreas fault system, within which they discern a fault zone and the fault itself. The fault system, which is 80 kilometres (50 miles) wide at the latitude of San Francisco, comprises all the immediate faults along the plate tectonic boundary, both onshore and offshore, most of which have their own names and histories; these include the Hayward fault, which runs parallel to the main San Andreas fault east of San Francisco, and which ruptured spectacularly in 1868. The much smaller San Andreas fault zone,

The San Andreas fault in the Carrizo Plain, central California.

varying in width from 0.5 to 0.8 kilometres, is the area of highly sheared rock. The San Andreas fault itself is the most recent break in the earth's crust that is discernible, and ranges in shape from a single or double furrow to a series of parallel fissures; those parts of the fault that do not break the surface are known as 'blind' faults. It is probably at its most visible, and best studied, in the forbidding Carrizo Plain.

The motives behind seismological research on the San Andreas fault are partly scientific and partly to anticipate and avoid a future earthquake-related disaster in one of the wealthiest areas of the world – the San Francisco Bay Area, Los Angeles and many other centres of population and industry, such as Silicon Valley, lie on top of or close to it. In 1906 the most destructive aspect of the San Francisco earthquake was the fire that followed it (as with the Great Kanto earthquake in Tokyo and Yokohama in 1923). 'The odds are respectable that Los Angeles or the Bay Area will be struck during California's long seasonal drought, when the whole surrounding landscape is primed to burn', wrote Marc Reisner in his final book, *A Dangerous Place: California's Unsettling Fate*, a chillingly detailed and convincing vision of what might happen in the event of another major earthquake. Reisner, as the author of *Cadillac Desert*, was an expert on water resources in the American West. In his view, 'The water supply systems will be damaged, perhaps even drained; when that happens, after fires are ignited – as they will be – a lot of what has survived the ground shaking will burn.'[1]

The attention of seismologists is focused on two stretches of the fault: the northern section, 435 kilometres (270 miles) long, which ruptured in 1906; and, even more critically, the southern section, 300 kilometres long, which has not slipped since an equally powerful earthquake at Fort Tejon in 1857. The long central section of the fault lying in between these 'locked' northern and southern sections is creeping steadily and does not store stress. At the Cienega Valley Winery near Hollister, which is built on top of the fault, the creep slowly pulls apart the building; but the fault seems to be good for the vineyard, which has won medals at wine fairs over many years. ('Crushed naturally by the

Map of the San
Andreas fault, showing
northern and southern
sections (solid line)
that slipped and
produced earthquakes
in 1906 and 1857.

San Andreas Fault' should be printed on the label of the winery's
bottles, suggests Fradkin jokingly.[2]) The creep means that it is
probably impossible for the entire San Andreas fault – all 1,300
kilometres of it from the Cape Mendocino Triple Junction in
the far north to the Salton Sea in the far south – to rupture in
a single earthquake. This would be a little like expecting to be
able to tear in half, all in one go, a creased newspaper with a
soggy patch part way along the crease.

In 1857 Los Angeles was only a small town, population
4,000, located 65 kilometres (40 miles) from the fault. Some of
its houses developed cracks but none was severely damaged. Two
people in the entire region of southern California were killed.
And that, apart from bad damage to Fort Tejon, was about all.
Compare the effects of the most recent major San Andreas earthquake centred on Loma Prieta, south of San Francisco, in 1989
– smaller in magnitude, at 7.0, than the magnitude 7.9 estimated
for the quakes of both 1857 and 1906. The 1989 quake happened
when the southernmost 40 kilometres (25 miles) of the northern

section of the San Andreas fault ruptured. There were 63 fatalities and nearly 4,000 people were injured; around 1,000 homes were destroyed and many more damaged; and at least $6 billion of damage was done, mainly in San Francisco (especially its Marina District) – some reports said a great deal more.

A particular cause for alarm is the pattern of seismicity along the San Andreas fault in recent decades. Tremors are frequent along a substantial part of its length (although not so much along the two sections that ruptured in 1857 and 1906). But the section lying closest to Los Angeles is eerily quiet, with barely the tiniest of tremors. When the fault finally ruptures, which is almost certain to happen during this century, will there be precursors, such as the swarms of tremors that preceded the magnitude-7.4 Chinese earthquake that struck Haicheng in 1975, which provoked virtually everyone affected to take refuge out of doors before the main shock? Or will there instead be a single, totally unexpected jolt, as in a second great Chinese earthquake in Tangshan in 1976, which took at least 250,000 lives?

A series of moderate-magnitude quakes near (but not exactly on) the San Andreas south of Los Angeles, where the fault reaches the Salton Sea, began to worry scientists from the late 1980s. In 1992 the quakes culminated in a magnitude-7.4 quake at Landers, soon followed by a magnitude-6.7 quake at Northridge in 1994. Are Californians witnessing a menacing build-up towards the Big One? No one has any clear idea: such a series of quakes may have made a major quake more likely in the next few decades, but it is also possible that by releasing stress they have diminished the likelihood.

The principal difficulty in choosing an answer is that the San Andreas fault does not properly obey the 'elastic rebound' model (dating from the 1906 quake) of how earthquakes are said to work. Consider fault temperature, for instance. Leaving aside the bursts of heat produced by actual rupture, one would naturally expect the temperature at the fault to be higher than it is away from it, since steady heat should be generated by friction as the two plates rub against each other (rather as heat is produced by rubbing one's hands together). 'However,' says the

Collapsed section of the Bay Bridge, San Francisco, caused by the Loma Prieta earthquake, 1989.

1990 United States Geological Survey (USGS) report on the
fault system,

> the frictional heating predicted for the process has never been
> detected. Thus, in spite of its importance to an understanding
> of both plate motion and earthquakes, the size of this fric-
> tional stress is still uncertain, even in order of magnitude.[3]

The forces measured at the fault are in fact completely cock-
eyed: in scientific terms, the stress is high-angle. Instead of
being aligned along the fault, the stress acts principally at right
angles to it, in a NE–SW orientation, instead of NW–SE, as expected. Instead of acting to shear the fault, the stress seems to
be trying to pull it apart. If this is correct, the San Andreas fault,
far from being strong, is actually remarkably weak.

There is other evidence to support this surprising conclusion.
Earthquakes do not produce the large drop in stress required by
the calculations based on the 'elastic rebound' model of a fault. If
they did, even a small earthquake would cause the ground to
move 90 metres (300 feet) at 40 kilometres (25 miles) per hour:
not even insects would survive! Formerly this was explained away
by saying that much of the initial stress remained in a fault after
a quake – hence the aftershocks. But studies of the San Andreas
fault at the time of the Loma Prieta earthquake in 1989 finally
disproved this theory. A USGS team compared the direction of
small shocks before and after the earthquake and found the
aftershocks to be oriented 'every which way', not in the direction of the earlier shocks. In other words, the earthquake had
dissipated virtually all the stress on the fault. They concluded
that the initial stress on the fault must have been lower than that
predicted by the model.

A further misfit between model and reality concerns the
speed of rupture. Obviously, scientists can rarely hope to observe
a rupture as it occurs. But eyewitness accounts suggest that the
process is much faster than 'elastic rebound' allows. The fault slips
much more easily than expected. In a report of a 7.2-magnitude
quake in Idaho in 1983, one side of a fault was seen to be shoved

1 metre in the air in just 1 second. If conventional friction had been restraining it, the slippage should have taken ten times as long.

Yet another suggestive line of evidence concerns the effect of historic earthquakes on precariously balanced rocks scattered across the landscape of southern California. There are many such boulders, which can be regarded as primitive strong-motion seismometers. Above a particular level of ground shaking in an earthquake, such rocks should topple over. The geologist James Brune and his colleagues have estimated the earthquake ground motion that would be required to topple the rocks through experiments with lifting equipment, at the same time as attempting to date the rocks through chemical analysis of their surface varnish and the level of certain isotopes created by the constant bombardment of cosmic rays. If such methods are accepted as valid (which is debated among seismologists), the surprising result is that the rocks have survived what are believed to have been major earthquakes in the region during the past 10,000 and more years. Presumably the ground shaking in these quakes was less than expected on the basis of the strong faults envisioned in the 'elastic rebound' model.

'Weak Faults: Breaking Out All Over' was a headline in the journal *Science* in a report on earthquake research in 1992. 'Earthquakes used to be simple', it warned at the outset, and promptly went on to quote a Stanford University geophysicist, Mark Zoback, with years of San Andreas experience: 'We fundamentally don't understand how earthquakes work. After all these years, we don't have a clue.'[4] Not every earthquake scientist is as gloomy as this, but all admit the severe limitations of the existing 'elastic rebound' model. 'Exactly how and when do faults fail? Why do earthquakes stop? How do ruptures travel along complicated fault zones?' are problems that have not yet been solved, writes Susan Hough in her book *Earthshaking Science: What We Know (and Don't Know) about Earthquakes*. 'Any presentation of earthquake basics inevitably raises almost as many questions as it answers.'[5]

Seth Stein teaches 'elastic rebound' to undergraduate students by attaching a rubber band to a box containing a bar of soap and attempting to pull it across a yoga mat. Pulling on the rubber band at first causes it to stretch elastically without moving the box until the point when the band's stretching force overcomes the friction between the box and the mat – when the box suddenly slips forward and the rubber band snaps back to its original length. 'This analogy goes to the heart of how faults and earthquakes work', writes Stein.[6] But those who are dissatisfied with 'elastic rebound' theory offer totally different models. As an example of how far thinking about earthquakes has changed (leaving aside the validity of the ideas), models of fault movement that have been seriously proposed include banana peels slipping slickly past each other; a melting ice cube that slides across a counter top when pushed from above rather than from the side (the direction of the force represents high-angle stress in real faults such as the San Andreas); and a wrinkle passing rapidly through a rug instead of the entire rug being clumsily tugged (carpet fitters have long used this principle). This last model is akin to the movement of defects in metal crystal lattices during metal dislocation and deformation.

Despite their diversity, all the models are agreed on one point: something comes between the sides of the fault and lubricates it, making it weak. 'Upward migration of fluids may trigger the occurrence of earthquakes', suggests a Caltech scientist, Thomas Heaton, in a significant survey of earthquake mechanisms.[7] At the temperatures and pressures 5–16 kilometres (3–10 miles) down, where the relatively shallow San Andreas earthquakes occur, the lubricant cannot be ground rock or clay, but it could be mineral fluids trapped in the fault when it was formed, or alternatively fluids pumped up from the more ductile regions below the fault. Talc, a hydrous magnesium silicate formed by the action of hydrothermal fluids on magnesium-rich serpentinite rocks, which is well known for its slipperiness, is a candidate. Probably there is more than coincidence to the fact that the San Andreas fault creeps in central California, where serpentinite rocks (and presumably talc) occur.

The lubricant might also be water: there seems to be plenty of water deep in a fault, judging from the appearance of faults exhumed by erosion. In fact, evidence from areas other than the San Andreas fault substantially supports the idea that water can lubricate faults. In the early 1960s, for instance, a series of earthquakes occurred near Denver in Colorado, where hitherto the natural seismicity had always been low. Between April 1962 and September 1963 local seismographic stations registered more than 700 epicentres with magnitudes of up to 4.3. Then there was a sharp decline in seismicity during 1964, followed by another series of quakes during 1965. It turned out that the US army was injecting contaminated water from weapons production at its Rocky Mountain arsenal northeast of Denver into a deep well, bored to a depth of about 3,660 metres (12,000 feet). Injection of the water began in March 1962 and ceased in September 1963 for a year. It resumed in September 1964 and finally ceased in September 1965. Residents of Denver, alarmed at the earthquakes, succeeded in stopping the army's method of disposal.

With the knowledge from this chance experiment in mind, the USGS began a designed experiment in 1969 at an oil field in Rangely, western Colorado. Using existing oil wells, water was injected into a well or pumped out at will and the pore pressure of the crustal rock was measured (that is, the pressure of fluid absorbed by the rock). At the same time an array of seismographs, specially installed in the area, monitored seismicity. There turned out to be an excellent correlation between higher fluid pore pressure and increase in seismicity. In both the Denver and Rangely cases, therefore – and at times in the controversial oil and gas extraction process known as 'fracking' (hydraulic fracturing) – it appears that water entered faults underground and lubricated them, causing earthquakes. Conceivably, the fact might be used to relieve stress selectively on a fault such as the San Andreas; if controlled small earthquakes could be triggered, large damaging ones might be prevented. The idea is potentially so hazardous, however – akin to the idea mentioned in the last chapter of 'spot welding' tectonic plates with underground nuclear bombs – that it is unlikely to be applied unless scientists' grasp of earthquake mechanism improves dramatically. But it might be worth trying in order to relieve rock stress in the construction of a dam.

Dams provide incontrovertible evidence that water can lubricate rock movement through so-called 'reservoir triggered seismicity'. The water probably causes earthquakes by infiltrating faults beneath the reservoir rather than by increasing the direct pressure on the rock. (Calculations show that this increase is fairly small, compared to normal rock pressures a few miles down.) Most large dams have not demonstrated increased seismicity when filled, but there have been a number of significant exceptions, a few of them big enough to be worrying.

The first was at Lake Mead, behind the Hoover Dam in Nevada-Arizona: earthquakes reached a peak there in 1940, after five years of impoundment (filling) of water, and then decreased. When Lake Kariba in Zambia was being filled between 1958 and 1963, there were hundreds more earthquakes per year than usual; the biggest, in September 1963, had a magnitude of 5.8. After that, activity declined. In Egypt, near the Aswan High Dam, an earthquake of magnitude 5.6 with aftershocks was reported in 1981. No significant earthquake had been measured in Upper Egypt since global seismology began at the turn of the century, nor did the historical record going back 3,000 years mention any large earthquake. The shock of 1981, with its epicentre below an extensive bay of Lake Nasser about 65 kilometres (40 miles) from the dam, was therefore probably an effect of the lake. It is likely that the very porous sandstones along the Nile have absorbed a huge volume of water, thereby creating large changes in pore pressure.

However, the most serious cases of what may be dam-related earthquakes have been in India and in China. At Koyna, in western India, the dam is in an area of low seismicity. Reports of shaking in the Koyna region became common after 1962 when impoundment of the reservoir began, and seismographs showed the earthquake hypocentres to be at shallow depths below the dam's Shivsagar Lake. During 1967 there were a number of sizeable quakes, climaxing in December with a magnitude-6.3 shock that caused damage to buildings, killed over 200 people and injured many more. A strong-motion seismograph in the dam gallery registered a massive sideways acceleration of 0.63

Zipingpu Dam in the Min River, Sichuan province, China.

times the acceleration due to gravity. The intensity of damage measured X on the Modified Mercalli Scale. In the Chinese province of Sichuan, by contrast, the earthquake occurred in an area known to be seismically active, though not at a high magnitude in recent decades. In 2008 a magnitude-7.9 earthquake in Sichuan killed almost 70,000 people and wiped out the town of Beichuan. What attracted attention from researchers was the proximity of the epicentre to the Zipingpu Dam. The dam was 5.5 kilometres (3.5 miles) from the epicentre and just half a kilometre from the fault that failed. The impoundment of the dam with 300 million tonnes of water was completed in 2006. Although there is no proof of any connection between the Indian dam, the Chinese dam and nearby earthquakes – an idea largely rejected by those involved in constructing and running the projects – a link seems probable in the Indian case, and at least possible in the Chinese one. Fan Xiao, a chief engineer of the Sichuan Geology and Mineral Bureau in neighbouring Chengdu, went on record in 2009 to urge more attention to the seismic risks in future dam-building projects. 'We should readjust our existing plans and take a more cautious attitude when planning projects,' he told *Science*. 'But I am pessimistic that many of these large-scale constructions will be cancelled, because of the strong economic interests that benefit hydropower developers and local governments.'[8]

Business interests in California have long played a key role in the state's relationship with the San Andreas fault. They have generally preferred obfuscation of the state's seismic risks to exposure by inquiry committees. A disturbing scientific report on the Hayward fault earthquake in 1868 – which seriously damaged San Francisco and lasted three times as long as the 1989 Loma Prieta quake – was never published. Apparently it was suppressed as a result of opposition from the city authorities and the chamber of commerce in San Francisco. So nothing was learnt from the earthquake of 1868 about how to build safely in the city. After the earthquake of 1906 a sustained effort was

Soldiers patrol as Market Street in San Francisco burns after the earthquake, 1906.

Emergency feeding
of homeless people in
San Francisco after
the earthquake, 1906.

made to blame the city's destruction on the fire rather than the earthquake, and this belief became firmly established. In the first place, building insurance policies generally covered fires and not earthquakes. Second, focusing on the fire deflected attention away from any long-term seismic risk to the city. Third, this view encouraged efforts to rebuild the city as it was before, as quickly as possible, without any expensive changes to the foundations and structural engineering of buildings. The San Francisco daily newspapers abetted the belief by publishing telegraphic reports of small tremors in the eastern United States, while omitting to report the stronger aftershocks in San Francisco itself.

Even the 1906 death toll was deliberately underestimated as 700 instead of the true figure of more than 3,000 people in San Francisco alone – as revealed by two local researchers, Gladys Hansen and Emmet Condon, in their 1989 book *Denial of Disaster*. Hansen's interest in the truth had been triggered in the 1960s when she was put in charge of the genealogy collection at the city's library. There she was regularly asked for a list of those who had died in 1906 and discovered that no such list existed. It took almost a century from the date of the earthquake before the higher-casualty figure became generally accepted.

'The policy of assumed indifference, which is probably not shared by any other earthquake district in the world, has continued to the present time and is accompanied by a policy of concealment', complained the distinguished geologist Grove Karl Gilbert in his presidential address to the American Association of Geographers in 1909. 'It is feared that if the ground of California has a reputation for instability, the flow of immigration will be checked, capital will go elsewhere, and business activity will be impaired.'[9]

In southern California, after the magnitude-6.4 Long Beach earthquake, 'the Panglossian Los Angeles City Council passed a resolution emphasizing the goodwill generated by the 1933 quake', notes Fradkin.[10] Many residents somehow convinced themselves that the Long Beach earthquake was southern California's equivalent of the great earthquake of 1906 in northern California. 'Though only a moderate earthquake', admitted Charles Richter, it ranked as a 'major disaster'. But at least, he added,

> This calamity had a number of good consequences. It put an end to efforts by incompletely informed or otherwise misguided interests to deny or hush up the existence of serious earthquake risk in the Los Angeles metropolitan area.[11]

A mixture of almost total ignorance about earthquakes and false optimism about human beings prevailed among the Californian public at the time. The journalist and social critic Carey McWilliams collected together some of the folk tales circulating in the local newspapers around Long Beach immediately after the 1933 event:

> That an automobile, while being driven along a boulevard in Long Beach, shook so hard that it lost all four tyres; that the undertakers in Long Beach didn't charge a penny for the 60 or more interments following the quake; that the quake was the first manifestation of the awful curse placed on Southern California by the Rev. Robert P. Shuler after its residents failed to elect him United States Senator; that sailors on vessels a mile or more off shore from Palos Verdes saw the hills (quite high) disappear from sight; that the bootleggers

of Long Beach saved hundreds of lives by their public-spirited donation of large quantities of alcohol to the medical authorities; that women showed the most courage during the quake and that men can't stand up under earthquakes; that the shock of the quake caused dozens of miscarriages in Long Beach, and that an earthquake will often cause permanent, and annoying, irregularities among women; that every building in Southern California that was not damaged by the quake is 'earthquake proof'; … [and finally] that the earthquake, followed by the appearance of a mighty meteor on 24 March, presages the beginning of the end.[12]

A famous folk tale from the earthquake of 1906 – probably inspired by biblical stories of the earth opening and swallowing cities – fooled even Gilbert, David Starr Jordan, the president of Stanford University (which lost its new geology building in the quake), and a number of newspaper journalists. Gilbert reported that a cow had been swallowed by a fissure on a ranch in Olema, just south of Point Reyes Station, leaving only its tail, which was then eaten by dogs. He had not seen the cow or the tail himself, and when he looked for a crack large enough to bury a cow, he failed to find it. Nevertheless, he said, 'the testimony on this point is beyond question'; the crack must have been caused by 'a temporary parting of the walls'. Probably the rancher, Payne Shafter, had played a practical joke on Gilbert and others. 'Shafter had a dead cow to bury, and along came the earthquake', writes Fradkin. 'He buried the cow and made up a good story for the bothersome newspaper reporters and geologists.'[13]

In California today, the 'assumed indifference' of most Californians – apart from seismologists, geophysicists, engineers, architects and insurance underwriters – still predominates. California has never lacked for cults, yet there is no Californian earthquake cult and curiously little Californian earthquake culture, with only the occasional novel, such as F. Scott Fitzgerald's *The Last Tycoon*, featuring a quake. Much more surprisingly, in a state that draws justifiable attention to its scenery, the

government makes scarcely any attempt to signpost the San Andreas fault for tourists as a natural feature as important in its own way as, say, the Grand Canyon in Arizona; only three such displays exist over its entire length. When Fradkin travelled the San Andreas in the 1990s and wrote about his experiences in his lively account, *Magnitude 8*, he asked: 'What does it feel like to live near, or on top of such a powerful force?' His honest answer was:

> Most people are unaware of its existence, since there is an almost total absence of signage, and damaging events are infrequent. Others give very little thought to its presence. These were the prevalent attitudes that I encountered along the fault line, where the transient nature of the populace does not lend itself to long-term memories.[14]

The film producers of Hollywood – alert as ever to making money from the public mood – must have sensed this public indifference, too. There are a couple of notable feature films about earthquakes in California: the disaster movie *Earthquake* (1974), starring Charlton Heston as an engineer, in which Los Angeles is destroyed by a great quake; and the dystopian *Escape from L.A.* (1996), where the city is also wrecked. Closer to reality, however, in the natural disasters section of the theme park of Universal Studios (which produced *Earthquake*) the visitor's experience of an earthquake is firmly situated in San Francisco, not Los Angeles. And on Sunset Boulevard, which lies either directly on top of the Hollywood fault or just north of it, there is no sign whatsoever to indicate the fault's ghostly presence. 'It's not an attraction', according to the tourist information centre run by the Los Angeles Convention and Visitors Bureau. With so much at stake, and so little certainty about when the 'Big One' will strike the city, it is only human to deny – or at least try to forget – the continual risks of cohabiting with the San Andreas fault system.

Poster for the disaster movie *Earthquake* (dir. Mark Robson, 1974), centred on a great earthquake in Los Angeles.

8 Prediction of the Unpredictable

The earthquake that shook Northridge, a neighbourhood of Los Angeles in the San Fernando Valley, in 1994, gave a disturbing idea of what might happen to Los Angeles in the event of a great earthquake. Although its magnitude was comparatively low at 6.7, the ground acceleration near its epicentre was one of the highest ever recorded by instruments in North America: 1.7 times the acceleration due to gravity. Half a century earlier, before the Second World War, the area affected had been mainly farmland. By the 1990s it had become densely developed. Parts of its extensive freeway system were spectacularly destroyed, garnering international media attention, but by sheer luck hardly any of its thousands of daily commuters died, because the earthquake struck at 4.31 a.m. A motorcycle officer from the Los Angeles Police Department was killed after his motorcycle plunged 12 metres (40 feet) from a collapsed interchange; when the interchange was reopened a year later, it was named in his honour. Overall, an estimated $20 billion of damage was done, making this the most costly earthquake disaster in US history. The sight of the destruction provoked the film director John Carpenter, a long-time resident of Los Angeles, into making his disaster movie *Escape from L.A.* on the grounds that 'we're living in Pompeii waiting for the volcano to blow and denying it', as he told the *Los Angeles Times*.[1]

Collapse of a freeway interchange following the Northridge earthquake, southern California, 1994.

Very shortly after the earthquake occurred, notes Susan Hough in *Earthshaking Science*, 'when the southern California earth science community was still abuzz with the frantic adrenaline rush

Film still from *Escape from L.A.* (dir. John Carpenter, 1996).

that accompanies large and destructive local earthquakes', someone asked 'an eminent seismologist' if anyone had predicted the earthquake. 'Not yet', he replied ironically.[2]

Earthquake prediction is a seductive mirage – forever beckoning but always out of reach. After a major earthquake, people on the fringes of seismology may claim to have successfully predicted it, and then go on to use their supposed 'track record' to predict a future event. Although professionals in the field can justifiably claim some success in predicting where major earthquakes will occur, the 'when' of such events eludes their predictive powers. Yet seismologists have quite often been seduced into making predictions. In 1923, as we know, Japan's leading seismologist, Omori, failed abysmally to predict the Great Kanto earthquake, whereas his colleague Imamura managed somewhat better: he got the epicentre (under Sagami Bay) right, and the timing correct to within a 50-year window beginning in 1905. But there was no reliable theory underlying this prediction. In the 1970s earthquake prediction seemed to gain some serious scientific credibility. A reputable US geologist predicted that a magnitude-8.4 earthquake in Peru would occur in late 1980 – a date he subsequently revised to June 1981. His prediction panicked the country yet turned out to be a false alarm. In 1989 a climatologist's prediction of a major earthquake in the American

Midwest on 3 December 1990 fell on fertile ground already prepared by seismologists concerned about the seismic potential of the region. People in Missouri spent $22 million on earthquake insurance. Again, nothing happened. On the other hand, in 2009, in Italy, following frequent tremors in the Abruzzo region, government scientists predicted that a major earthquake was unlikely. A week later, a disastrous magnitude-6.3 quake struck L'Aquila. The scientists were later taken to court by the city's authorities, as mentioned in chapter One. One of the survivors, a surgeon who lost his wife and daughter in the quake, stated bitterly: 'That night, all of the old people in L'Aquila, after the first shock, went outside and stayed outside for the rest of the night. Those of us who are used to using the Internet, television, science – we stayed inside.'[3]

Perhaps the sole earthquake prediction that enjoys at least a modicum of credibility among scientists is that of the Haicheng earthquake in China in 1975. No large earthquake – and relatively few moderate ones – had occurred in the Liaoning province of Manchuria for over 100 years when, in early 1974, minor tremors began to increase. In the first five months of the year Chinese scientists measured five times the normal number. They discovered, too, that much of the region had been uplifted and tilted to the northwest, and that the strength of the earth's magnetic field was increasing in the area. They also observed anomalous underground electrical current readings and well water levels. The State Seismological Bureau in Beijing issued a forecast: Liaoning should expect a moderate to strong earthquake within two years. On 22 December there was another burst of tremors. The forecast became more focused: to expect an earthquake of magnitude 5.5–6 somewhere in the region of Yingkou, a major industrial port, during the first six months of 1975.

All over the affected area, animals started to behave strangely. Snakes awoke from hibernation prematurely and lay frozen in the snow; rats appeared in groups so agitated that they did not fear human beings; small pigs chewed off their tails and ate them. Wells began to bubble. A swarm of tremors – 500 were recorded in 72 hours – culminated in a magnitude-5.1 jolt at 7.51 a.m. on

4 February 1975. A number of moderate shocks then followed, but by the evening the seismic activity was dying down.

Nevertheless, local party officials – after being vigorously spurred on by the head of the Earthquake Office in Yingkou County, a former army officer named Cao Xianqing, at an emergency meeting at 8.15 a.m. – decided on an evacuation. At 2 p.m. on 4 February three million people were ordered to leave their homes and spend the night outdoors in straw shelters and tents. Without panicking, the citizens of southern Liaoning province obeyed. The outside temperature was already many degrees below freezing. In Haicheng County there was less sense of urgency from observers of the tremors, and the evacuation was not so extensive.

During the day Cao Xianqing predicted that the earthquake would occur before 8 p.m., and furthermore that it would be of magnitude 7 at 7 p.m. and of magnitude 8 at 8 p.m. At 7.36 p.m. the earthquake struck – with a magnitude of 7.3. Sheets of light flashed through the sky, the earth heaved; 4.5-metre (15-foot) jets of water and sand shot into the air. Roads and bridges buckled; rural communes tumbled down. Most buildings in Yingkou and neighbouring Haicheng – a town of 90,000 people – were wrecked. But because of the evacuation of people from their homes, and because the quake came in the evening – when large masonry structures such as schools, office buildings and factories were empty – instead of tens of thousands of deaths there were relatively few: some 2,000 fatalities from the earthquake, fires and hypothermia combined.

A year and a half later, in Tangshan – an industrial and mining centre with a population of a million, 120 kilometres (75 miles) east of Beijing – the people were much less fortunate. The magnitude-7.5 earthquake, larger than in Haicheng, struck at 3.42 a.m., unannounced by foreshocks. The few precursors that scientists had observed, such as strange lights the night before the quake and disturbances in well water levels, were either insufficient for a prediction or had been ignored by the authorities. Unlike Liaoning, the Tangshan area had not been selected for special monitoring by the State Seismological Bureau. Tangshan

Row of trees offset
1.5 metres (5 feet)
by the Tangshan
earthquake, China,
1976, photographed 6
years after the quake.

was asleep in bed. At least 250,000 people, perhaps as many as 750,000, were killed; the actual figure was officially concealed. It was the worst earthquake death toll of the twentieth century.

According to the party line emanating from Beijing in 1975, 'The Haicheng earthquake was successfully predicted, saving untold thousands of lives.'[4] A careful later investigation by Kelin Wang, Qi-Fu Chen, Shi-hong Sun and Andong Wang, published in 2006 in the *Bulletin of the Seismological Association of America*, is more equivocal. It accepts that the energetic actions of Cao Xianqing in Yingkou were crucial in saving lives. But it shows that he acted more from gut instinct than from any scientific theory in predicting the details of the earthquake's timing and magnitude. 'This patently absurd aspect of the forecast was apparently based on some sort of extrapolation of foreshock activity', writes Hough in her study of earthquake prediction, *Predicting the Unpredictable*.[5] Cao himself told interviewers that he had based the forecast on a book, *Serendipitous Records of Yingchuan*, which stated that heavy autumn rains would certainly be followed by a winter earthquake. Observing the heavy autumn rains of 1974 and the escalating seismic activity in this period, he predicted an earthquake before what he thought was the official end of the Chinese winter at 8 p.m. on 4 February. But since he got this time wrong – the official end was actually 7 p.m. – by his reckoning the earthquake was half an hour late!

The fact that earthquake prediction as a science has such a chequered history is hardly to be wondered at. 'One may compare it to the situation of a man who is bending a board across his knee and attempts to determine in advance just where and when the cracks will appear', wrote Charles Richter in 1958. 'All claims to predict the future have a hold on the imagination; it is not surprising that even qualified seismologists have been led astray by the will-o'-the-wisp of prediction.'[6] About the predictors themselves, Richter wrote bluntly in some unpublished notes in 1976:

> What ails them is exaggerated ego plus imperfect or ineffective education, so that they have not absorbed one of the fundamental rules of science – self-criticism. Their wish for attention distorts their perception of facts, and sometimes leads them on into actual lying.[7]

Scientists' hopes for long-term prediction are pinned mainly on a cyclical concept arising from the 'elastic rebound' model: fault stress is thought to build at a constant rate and be dissipated abruptly in regularly occurring ruptures. We shall return to this idea. In the short term, by contrast, everything depends on precursors and, by extension, the instrumentation, personnel and social organization necessary to observe and measure them. Possible precursors include foreshocks, changes in ground strain, tilt, elevation and resistivity, alterations in the local magnetic and gravitational fields, shifting of groundwater levels, the emission of radon gas, deep sounds, flashes of light and the peculiar behaviour of animals. Some of these precursors appear months or even years ahead of a large earthquake; others only in the days and hours before it strikes.

Foreshocks are the most useful. Unfortunately, they frequently do not happen, at least not in the period immediately

Earthquake 'lights'
during the Matsuhiro
earthquakes, Japan,
1966.

before the quake. There were none in Tokyo in mid-1923, none in Tangshan in 1976, practically none in Gujarat in 2001 and none in a typical major Californian quake, the one at San Fernando in 1971 (magnitude 6.5). A later review of micro-earthquakes in the area during the 30 months leading up to the San Fernando quake showed, however, that a drop in the speed of P waves by 10–15 per cent had taken place, followed by a return to normal speed just before the quake. A rather similar phenomenon had been observed by Soviet seismologists after detailed monitoring of small and large earthquakes in Tajikistan during the 1950s and '60s: they found that the ratio of P to S wave speed dropped for a variable period and then suddenly returned to normal just before a major quake. US monitoring, spurred on by the Soviet results, seemed to confirm this general picture, and for a while optimism about earthquake prediction reached a high. *Scientific American*, introducing an article on the subject in 1975, went so far as to declare: 'Recent technical advances have brought this long-sought goal within reach. With adequate funding several countries, including the us, could achieve reliable long-term and short-term forecasts in a decade.'[8] But subsequent extensive measurement of seismicity at the San Andreas fault revealed no such general predictable behaviour by P waves. If the method does prove useful in prediction, it will work – like so many other methods in seismology – only locally, within particular geological conditions that have been extensively studied over a sufficiently long period.

This is certainly true of attempts to understand uplift and subsidence of the ground. On 16 June 1964 a major earthquake struck the coastal town of Niigata in western Japan, its epicentre just off the coast at Awashima Island. There was a sudden subsidence of the coastline by 15–20 centimetres (6–8 inches). This in itself was unremarkable, but when plotted on a graph of land elevation in relation to mean sea level since 1898, the sudden slump was shown to have followed a gradual rise in the land opposite Awashima Island at the rate of nearly 2 millimetres (0.1 inch) a year. The fact was, of course, noticed only after the earthquake. By keeping a constant watch on the elevation of likely trouble-spots, with the help of laser-ranging devices and the satellites of the Global Positioning System (GPS), uplift may eventually turn into a useful indicator of a coming earthquake.

But even if uplift can be successfully quantified in advance of a disaster, there remains the awkward question of interpretation. The most celebrated example is the 'Palmdale Bulge', the uplift of an area of southern California centred on Palmdale, some 72 kilometres (45 miles) north of Los Angeles, and extending 160 kilometres along the San Andreas fault. The uplift, measured from the 1960s (that is, before the advent of the GPS), was said to amount to a striking 35 centimetres (13.75 inches), though subsequent studies suggested this figure had arisen from errors in the measurements, leading to heated arguments in the 1970s about whether or not the bulge really existed. If it did, what did

Ground movements
before and after the
Niigata earthquake,
Japan, 1964.

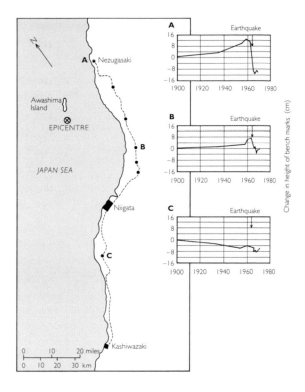

overleaf:
Highway cut
showing geological
folding in the San
Andreas fault, near
Palmdale, California.

it signify – perhaps the imminence of an earthquake in the area
(which lies on the southern section of the fault, the 300 kilometres that have not slipped since 1857)? The final verdict seems
to be that there is solid evidence of some uplift in the Palmdale
area, and that it is a consequence of the Kern County earthquake
of 1952, notes Hough. 'But as a harbinger of doom it [has] clearly
not lived up to expectations.'[9]

If a trio of Greek scientists – two solid-state physicists and
an electronics engineer – are correct, studies of the electrical
resistivity of the ground might throw some light on phenomena
like the Palmdale uplift and also provide a method of earthquake
prediction. The VAN method, named after its inventors, Panayotis
Varotsos, Caesar Alexopoulos and Kostas Nomikos, is based on a
fact first reported by John Milne in a paper of 1898 given before
Britain's Royal Society. Ahead of a powerful earthquake, the natural electrical currents that circulate and fluctuate in the ground

(telluric currents) are disturbed, and hence the resistivity of the ground alters. Previous efforts to detect this so-called Seismic Electrical Signal (SES) and use it for prediction had failed in many countries, and the approach was abandoned. But the Greek scientists took it up in the 1980s and claimed substantial results: during 1988 and 1989 they predicted the location and magnitude of seventeen earthquakes around Greece with some success.

The VAN method is highly controversial, though it has some scientific supporters all over the world. One difficulty, common to seismology as a whole, is that each area of the world presents unique problems of data interpretation. Another is the long time (decades) required to calibrate a network of VAN stations in areas where, unlike Greece, tremors are uncommon. A third difficulty is the lack of a satisfactory explanation of the SES. But the most serious difficulty is that the SES, according to the VAN hypothesis, is not universally present during earthquakes but detectable only at certain 'sensitive sites'. As a consequence, 'no amount of negative evidence – the absence of the SES prior to large earthquakes – can ever disprove the hypothesis,' writes an unconvinced Hough, 'because any and all negative results can be dismissed as having been recorded at insensitive sites.'[10]

Unlike changes in resistivity, the presence of abnormal animal behaviour before some earthquakes has yet to be proven by a controlled experiment. Researchers have shown no correlation between cockroach activity and impending earthquakes, and no response from cows wearing earthquake sensors – even during the earthquake itself! There is a correlation between the number of lost pet ads and major storms (during which animals may run away), but no correlation between the number of such ads and major earthquakes. The design of animal-oriented earthquake experiments encounters an obvious difficulty, compounded by the fact that seismologists are instinctively sceptical about anecdotal reports, and prefer scarce research funding to be spent on more potentially productive investigations.

Nonetheless, there is ample evidence that animals may perceive an earthquake coming, as we saw in Liaoning province in 1975. Reports exist from all over the world, dating back to the earliest times, and are documented by Helmut Tributsch in his book *When the Snakes Awake*. Plutarch mentions a rabbit having had a premonition of an earthquake in Sparta in 469 BC, and Pliny the Elder describes something similar in his *Natural History*. Immanuel Kant noted of the Lisbon earthquake of 1755:

> The cause of earthquakes seems to spread its effect even into the surrounding air. An hour earlier, before the earth is being shaken, one may perceive a red sky and other signs of an altered composition of the air. Animals are taken with fright shortly before it. Birds flee into houses, rats and mice crawl out of their holes.[11]

Before the earthquake in Tokyo in 1923, catfish – the mischievous *namazu* of tradition – were seen to jump agitatedly in ponds, and could be caught in bucketfuls. In China the appearance of panicky rats (observed in the Haicheng earthquake) is an officially designated precursor. In May 1974, according to a scientific report, it saved the lives of a family in Yunnan province. A housewife had found rats running around her house since 5 May. On the night of 10 May they were so noisy she got up to hit them. Then she suddenly recalled a visit to an exhibition on earthquakes and evacuated the house. The following morning a magnitude-7.1 earthquake actually occurred, and the house collapsed.

Explanations of these and thousands of other reported instances may involve better-than-human sensitivity among animals to vibrations and sounds, electrical and magnetic fields and the odour of leaking gases. An electrical explanation – perhaps exposure to charged clouds of particles emitted by the ground – seems the most likely. If the mechanism were ever to be established, and an analogous, affordable detection instrument designed, then animals would no longer be needed for prediction – just as canaries are no longer needed to detect gases in mineshafts.

Long-term earthquake forecasting is much less successful – and potentially a great deal more hazardous – than long-term weather forecasting. Geological processes are so slow that prediction, even on the basis of a century of data, is like trying

to predict tomorrow's weather on the basis of one minute's observation. Until the arrival of plate tectonic theory in the 1960s, about all that could confidently be said was that earthquakes mostly would occur where they had previously occurred. Today's theory focuses this statement a little by suggesting that the longer the period since an earthquake has occurred, the more likely that place is to experience a quake. Many scientists also reckon that the size of the quake increases with increased time of quiescence.

At Pallett Creek, for instance, 55 kilometres (34 miles) northeast of Los Angeles, the geologist Kerry Sieh dug a trench into the San Andreas fault and revealed well-differentiated strata of silt, sand and peat that appear to have been disturbed by a series of large earthquakes over the past 1,400 years. Using carbon dating,

Chinese government posters depicting animals sensing the coming of an earthquake.

Sieh established the following dates for these earth movements, all but one of them approximate: 1857, 1745, 1470, 1245, 1190, 965, 860, 665, 545. The greatest interval is 275 years, the smallest 55 years, while the average is 160 years. Will southern California experience its next large earthquake during the next decade or merely during this century? The Pallett Creek recurrence interval is clearly too variable for any meaningful prediction. In northern California, on the Hayward fault, the situation seems slightly clearer. Another geologist, Jim Lienkaemper, has excavated trenches that show twelve large (approximately magnitude-7) earthquakes during the past 1,650 years – the latest in 1868 – with an average recurrence interval of 140 years over the last five of these quakes. But this is still not sufficient evidence to predict the timing of the next big earthquake on the Hayward Fault – as the experience of seismologists in Parkfield shows.

Parkfield (population 37), situated on the San Andreas fault halfway between Los Angeles and San Francisco, was for some years in the late 1980s and early '90s the self-styled 'Earthquake Capital of the World' where the earth allegedly 'Moves for You'. It boasted the only officially endorsed earthquake prediction in the United States. The recurrence interval seemed to be about 22 years: moderate earthquakes were reported there in 1857 and 1881 and were scientifically recorded in 1901, 1922, 1934 and 1966 (the last serendipitously observed by seismographs that had been deployed to monitor an underground nuclear explosion in Alaska). In 1985 the USGS announced that there was a 95 per cent probability of a magnitude-6 earthquake occurring at Parkfield before the end of 1992.

Unfortunately, seven years and $18 million later, the area had proved notable chiefly for its seismic *in*activity. The largest quake was one of magnitude 4.5 in October 1992. The USGS promptly issued a warning that the expected magnitude-6 quake might follow within 72 hours. The California Office of Emergency Services set up a mobile operations centre outside the Parkfield Café. Fire engines stood ready in nearby towns, and residents laid in extra supplies of water. Helicopters from four or five television stations hovered overhead, and reporters from dozens of newspapers arrived on the scene. But there was no sign of the earthquake.

It finally arrived in 2004, 37 years after the last moderate one in 1966. Apart from the fault breaking from south to north, rather than the other way around as predicted, the extent of the fault break and the earthquake's magnitude were as expected. But as an example of a prediction, it has to be regarded as a very qualified success, at best. The Parkfield prediction experiment, combined with failures in other areas of prediction, has re-inforced the scepticism of the majority of seismologists: none of them now shares the confidence about earthquake prediction common in the 1970s. Consider a survey of predictions of Pacific Ring earthquakes made by four geophysicists in 1979. They had defined segments of plate boundaries that had not experienced large earthquakes for 30 years as 'seismic gaps', having a high potential for a large earthquake. The survey of the 37 earthquakes with magnitude 7 that occurred in the north Pacific during the post-1979 decade showed that four quakes occurred in the pos-tulated high-potential seismic gaps, sixteen in zones predicted to have intermediate potential, and seventeen in zones that should have low potential. The fit between fact and prediction would actually have been better had the zones been assigned their potentials randomly. Would the prediction's success improve if only the largest earthquakes were considered, these being best explained by the 'elastic rebound' model? Apparently not: of the nine earthquakes of magnitude 7.5 or greater, one was in the high-potential zone, three in the intermediate-potential zone and five in the low-potential zone. 'The apparent failure of the gap model is surprising, given its intuitive good sense', com-mented a report in *Nature*. 'It may be that seismicity in some regions is quasiperiodic, whereas in others it clusters.'[12]

The whole field of earthquake prediction is plainly wide open for speculation. Many predictions are made by unscientific and pseudoscientific means, and most of these are ignored. But occasionally, for reasons that are not always clear, one of them catches on and causes panic. This is what happened in Decem-ber 1989 when a self-taught US climatologist, Iben Browning, predicted that a subtle bulging of the earth caused by the gravitational pull of the sun and the moon – calculated by astronomers to peak on 3 December 1990 – would trigger a catastrophic earthquake in the Mississippi Valley, comparable to the earthquakes of 1811–12 around New Madrid, Missouri. In addition to having a PhD (in zoology) and the support of the director of Southeast Missouri State University's Earthquake Information Center, Browning was said – by the *New York Times*, no less – to have forecast the Loma Prieta earthquake of 17 October 1989 'a week in advance'.[13] The *San Francisco Chronicle* stated: 'He missed by just 6 hours hitting the Oct. 17 San Francisco quake on the nose in a forecast published in 1985 and by only 5 minutes in an update a week before the disaster.'[14] As the director of the Bay Area Earthquake Preparedness Project later remarked, 'these things have a life of their own.'[15]

The prediction caused a frenzy for months in the Midwest, and on the predicted day itself the governor of Missouri and a national media circus descended on New Madrid. The public reaction was not much affected by rational arguments, such as those of a committee of seismologists who examined Browning's Loma Prieta claim in a video-recording and transcript and found it to be baseless, or the fact that the supportive Missouri seismologist, despite having a PhD in geophysics, was known to believe in psychic phenomena. In a short story about the area published a decade later, 'A Comparative Seismology' by Jacob Appel, a conman posing as a USGS seismologist tells a lonely older woman: 'The New Madrid fault's been dormant for nearly 200 years. Seismic tension building by the day. That's why you don't feel any action – there hasn't been any. But there will be eventually, Miss Silver. You have my scientific guarantee.'[16] She believes him, takes up his offer of escape from the coming catastrophe, and loses a lot of money.

The genuine scientific community could probably have scotched the prediction at the start, but it failed to act in time. This was partly because it did not take the forecast seriously, partly because of its general lack of confidence in the scientific approach to the subject, especially in regard to earthquakes in the Mississippi Valley (as opposed to the better-monitored California), and partly because of internal politics between federal agencies such as the USGS and university-based seismologists. Seth Stein, who is a professor of geological sciences at Northwestern University, refused to be drawn into the circus. Yet he admits in his thought-provoking and balanced book on earthquake hazard in the Midwest, *Disaster Deferred*, that scientists bear some responsibility for the hyperbolic public response in 1989–90:

> Browning's prediction was the spark that set off prepared firewood. The firewood was what federal and state agencies and even some university scientists had told the public about past earthquakes and future hazard. Much of this was wildly exaggerated to the point of being embarrassing.[17]

A decade earlier, Brian Brady, a bona fide geologist studying quake-like rock bursts in mines, had made a notorious prediction that a giant earthquake would strike Peru in June 1981. Rock bursts occur when mining reduces the confining pressure on neighbouring rock. Brady's examination of rocks as they fractured in the laboratory had convinced him of the existence of a 'clock' in the fracture process: once started, it would inexorably run on and produce an earthquake, its ticks being bursts of moderate foreshocks. Given the requisite historical and current seismicity data, Brady said that he could tell exactly when the quake would occur.

Fellow geophysicists refused to accept the theory that the small-scale (microscopic) process of rock fracture and the large-scale (macroscopic) mechanism of earthquakes were basically the same, 'scale invariant' in scientific language, since faults, unlike mine walls, always remain under enormous confining pressure. They said so formally through the National Earthquake Evaluation Prediction Council in early 1981, after what amounted to a 'trial' of Brady before his peers. What they did not say, but certainly perceived, was that if his theory were right after all, it would mean wholesale realignment of earthquake research and funding towards laboratory work, away from field research.

The prediction had been news before; now it was headline news. But Brady refused to withdraw it, and so it became thoroughly entangled in Peruvian–US politics. The Peruvian president, government and scientific community were taking it seriously, while in Washington, DC, and at the US Geological Survey and the US Bureau of Mines, several different groups were vying to use the prediction for their own ends. The people of Peru, 66,000 of whom had died in an earthquake as recently as 1970, became more and more jittery as 28 June 1981 approached. The capital, Lima, became eerily quiet: many people, both rich and poor, left town for the weekend.

Nothing happened. But that does not devalue the thinking behind the prediction. The scientist concerned was not a crank, but he became obsessed with his model and pushed it too far. His scientific critics, lacking a sound theory of their own, were in a weak position. In defending himself shortly before the date of the prediction, Brady wrote:

> Many within the seismological community are currently infatuated with simple fault models made more complex by the addition of asperities (hard zones along the fault surface) which tend to inhibit free body motion along the fault; an earthquake occurs once the asperities are broken … I believe we need to address the fundamental problem of *how* the fault gets there in the first place.[18]

It was a prescient remark. Only now have seismologists begun to face this challenge head on. One of them compared himself with rueful candour to an eighteenth-century physician, 'who although lacking understanding of disease is compelled to do something and so prescribes bleeding'. The scientific problem, he remarked, is likely to get worse before it gets better: our expanding knowledge of the earth, derived from the extraordinary sophistication of new instrumentation, has ironically 'served to magnify our lack of understanding'.[19] Perhaps no earthquakes illustrate the truth of this remark better than those of the American Midwest. What is the origin and nature of the invisible intraplate faulting that produces such 'forbidden' earthquakes? Thanks to the extraordinarily accurate GPS surveys of the New Madrid area of Missouri which were launched in the early 1990s, we now know that the North American plate shows less than 2 millimetres (0.08 inches) of movement per year, as compared with an average of about 36 millimetres per year for the San Andreas fault. In other words, it is virtually stationary. Does this mean that another large intraplate earthquake like those of 1811–12 is in the offing, or rather the opposite: that the area should be considered seismically inactive? The stakes are high for scientists, government agencies and residents; the debate is intense; but the truth, as ever with earthquake prediction, is likely to remain elusive for many years to come.

9 Designing against Death

While scientists from various specialities investigate and theorize about earthquakes and earthquake prediction, what can governments, institutions and individuals do to protect themselves from the seismic menace? Nearly half the world's big cities now lie in areas at risk from earthquakes. In Cairo, in 1992, there was a comparatively minor earthquake (magnitude 5.8) with its epicentre 35 kilometres (22 miles) south of the city centre and a mere 10 kilometres south of Old Cairo. Even so, the quake killed 545 Egyptians, injured some 6,500 and made 50,000 homeless, as well as completely destroying 350 buildings and severely damaging 9,000 others, including 350 schools, 216 mosques (the upper part of one of the minarets of al-Azhar collapsed) and ancient monuments such as the Great Pyramid at Giza, from which a large block rolled to the ground. Part of the reason for the disproportionate loss of life and structural damage was that Cairo had not experienced a destructive earthquake for a century and a half; the previous one had been in 1847. Thus the city had no building regulations in place to reduce damage by earthquakes and no contingency plan for the inhabitants in the event of a quake. Most of those who perished were the impoverished tenants of poorly constructed apartments or children crushed in the stampede to escape collapsing schoolrooms. Yet, at the same time, large parts of the city with better-constructed buildings were left untouched. As seismologists like to say: 'Earthquakes don't kill people; buildings do.' In the terrible Tangshan earthquake of 1976, 'the safest place to be by far was underground'[1];

Earthquake destruction, Old Cairo, Egypt, 1992.

of the roughly 10,000 miners beneath the city at the time, only seventeen perished, unlike their unfortunate families above ground. In Port-au-Prince, Haiti's capital, in the great earthquake of 2010, the death toll was particularly high because many buildings pancaked as a result of their supporting columns being made of sub-standard concrete or cinder blocks lacking adequate steel reinforcement. Around the globe, hundreds of millions of lives are now at permanent risk from earthquakes, along with countless billions of dollars' worth of property; and the numbers and amounts are certain to continue rising.

By contrast with Cairo, Port-au-Prince and indeed almost all of the cities at seismic risk, in Japan's capital city, Tokyo, where earth tremors are a fact of everyday life, a barrage of scientific instruments is in place to monitor aspects of the many faults that may affect the metropolitan area. These are connected to a high-tech control centre. Since 1977 an emergency committee of scientists has been permanently ready to respond to unexpected movements of the crust and advise the Japanese government on whether to issue an alert. The government has designated evacuation areas and briefed the population through heavy publicity; every 1 September, the anniversary of the Great Kanto earthquake of 1923, there are city-wide earthquake drills. Stringent building regulations have long been in force. Most major buildings have been retrofitted against earthquakes and new ones have routinely been constructed over many years to withstand the maximum possible shaking. Tokyo's skyscrapers and tower blocks are supposed to be the safest buildings in the city; indeed, office workers and residents are advised to stay inside them in an earthquake. They are no longer to rush out and risk being cut by flying glass or killed by one of the shop signs that hang above the streets.

And yet a little probing of these claims shows that many loopholes remain, and, more seriously, how vastly more vulnerable a modern city is than the Tokyo of 1923. What about the bullet trains, which travel at maximum speeds of 240–300 kilometres per hour (150–185 mph)? Train braking systems triggered by seismographs can give the bullet trains some seconds of advance warning of a coming shock wave and bring them screeching to a halt. This is what happened after the Tohoku-Oki earthquake and tsunami in 2011, when 27 bullet trains avoided derailment by applying emergency braking nine seconds before the shaking began, and 70 seconds before the most violent shocks. But will the brakes react fast enough if a train happens to be close to the epicentre of a severe Tokyo earthquake? What about the refinery and chemical complex built on soft reclaimed mud beside Tokyo Bay, the new tower blocks built there against expert advice, and the Hamaoka nuclear power plant, built in the 1970s

Annual earthquake drill, Tokyo, on 1 September – the day of the Great Kanto earthquake in 1923.

near the junction of two tectonic plates, 200 kilometres (125 miles) southwest of Tokyo? (This plant was eventually shut down, after the Fukushima Daiichi nuclear disaster following the Tohoku-Oki earthquake.) What about rampant cost-cutting and long-term corruption in the construction industry – a killer in Cairo in 1992 – which was so tellingly suggested by Akira Kurosawa in his classic film of 1960 *The Bad Sleep Well*? What will happen to electricity cables, gas mains, water mains, telephone and computer lines, communications in general? And who will coordinate the rescue efforts and cut through the bureaucratic rivalries that bedevil emergency planning? The damage and the official response in the aftermath of the unpredicted Kobe earthquake of 1995 and the unpredicted Tohoku-Oki earthquake of 2011 are not reassuring. In Kobe the supposedly earthquake-resistant Hangshin highway collapsed as a result of a maximum ground acceleration twice the size of the estimated figure for the Great Kanto earthquake. Other collapsed structures in Kobe revealed shoddy construction due to corrupt or sloppy building practices.

If the casual questioning of ordinary Japanese people means anything, most of those living in Tokyo do not truly accept that such a disaster could happen to their city. In the early 1990s a 27-year-old fashion designer, who moved to the capital to make his career, told the journalist Peter Hadfield, author of *Sixty Seconds That Will Change the World*: 'I don't know how many people will be killed. A million? A billion? I really don't know. It's not the sort of thing I ever talk about with my friends. I know an earthquake is possible, but deep in my heart I can't really believe it.' A 25-year-old businessman working for an international food company in Tokyo was a bit more realistic: 'I'm not so worried about it. I don't talk about it so much with my friends – only sometimes, when we're driving through a tunnel and I might make a joke about it. I don't know how many people will die. It depends on the severity of the earthquake. Maybe two million?' According to Hadfield, 'The majority of ordinary Japanese I spoke to during the course of researching this book had the feeling that, although they know and have been told that a major quake is coming, they still find the reality of such an event hard to believe.'[2]

Aerial view of the damage to the Fukushima Daiichi nuclear power plant, Japan, 2011, caused by a tsunami following the Tohoku-Oki earthquake.

On the other side of the Pacific those living on the San Andreas fault are equally fatalistic, or perhaps more so. After the San Francisco earthquake of 1906 the California Earthquake Investigation Commission set up by the state's governor received little help in gathering information from San Franciscans. One member of the commission, a geologist from Stanford University, later recalled:

> We were advised and even urged over and over again to gather no such information, and above all not to publish it. 'Forget it', 'the less said, the sooner mended', and 'there hasn't been any earthquake', were the sentiments we heard on all sides.[3]

The gleaming new San Francisco that emerged from the ashes of the old city – which was showcased to the world at the Panama-Pacific International Exposition in 1915 – was in fact structurally less sound than the pre-1906 city. Not until 1948, after much debate and the experience of the destructive Long Beach earthquake in 1933, did California impose minimal seismic design requirements. And not until 1990, after the Loma Prieta earthquake, did the state issue a detailed plan of what should happen in the event of an earthquake warning. At the same time insurance companies prospered as anxious householders who had previously avoided taking out earthquake insurance finally signed up for it. Yet even those with the most knowledge of earthquakes – scientists – are divided as to whether such insurance is worth the high premium and enormous deductible (excess). Stanford University – badly hit by the 1906 earthquake – took earthquake insurance from 1980 to 1985, but then dropped it after being offered a policy with a premium of $3 million per year, a $100

Statue of geologist Louis Agassiz at Stanford University, California, toppled by the San Francisco earthquake, 1906.

million deductible, and coverage for only $125 million loss above the deductible. In the 1989 earthquake, without any insurance, the university suffered a loss of some $160 million. The journalist Philip Fradkin, when researching *Magnitude 8* in the late 1990s, learnt from a long-time member and chairman of the California Seismic Safety Commission and worldwide expert on seismic hazard, Lloyd Cluff, that Cluff himself did not bother with earthquake insurance on his older house in San Francisco because the amount of the deductible made the insurance pointless. In southern California Hiroo Kanamori, Caltech's director of the seismology laboratory at Pasadena and one of the world's leading seismologists, did not bother with insurance either. Kanamori said: 'My personal way of dealing with earthquakes is that I want to reduce the worry I have. I live in a relatively inexpensive home, a cheap house, really, so that the loss will be limited. I am very happy about it.'[4] Not only did Kanamori carry no earthquake insurance; his house was not even retrofitted against earthquakes, unlike many older houses and other buildings in California.

The Loma Prieta quake was, as we know, the third major earthquake to strike San Francisco. The first one, on the Hayward fault in 1868, made people aware of the dangers of building on land reclaimed from San Francisco Bay, even though the official report on the earthquake seems to have been suppressed. Notwithstanding, more than a century later, in 1989, some of the most serious damage was in the city's Marina District, which was built on land reclaimed from the bay and used for the Panama-Pacific International Exposition. Bits of charred wood and pieces of imitation travertine – presumably from the fire of 1906 and the broken-up debris of the 1915 exposition – were ejected in sand boils in the Marina District when the ground liquefied. In 1991 the *Bulletin of the Seismological Society of America* came out with a special issue on the Loma Prieta earthquake: 800 pages of densely written technical description and analysis. In their introduction, the editors felt constrained to warn:

> Certainly, the Loma Prieta earthquake is a reminder that
> earthquakes do not have to occur where we want them to

occur or forecast them to occur and that our understanding of how and why earthquakes occur and recur, even along the best studied active crustal fault in the world, is rudimentary and incomplete . . . The effects of earthquake strong ground motion on unreinforced masonry, soft first storeys, decayed timbers, bad foundations, hydraulic fill and young Bay mud hardly qualify as news, especially in San Francisco where these 'lessons' had all been learned in 1906 if not before. Indeed, the principal lesson of the Loma Prieta earthquake seems to be that the American public, even in earthquake country, is surprisingly uninformed about even the basics of earthquake occurrence, hazards, and risk; the latest reminder of this is the enormous nonsense, much of it news-media generated, surrounding Iben Browning's bogus prediction for a major earthquake in the New Madrid seismic zone during the first week of December 1990. Until there is a permanent national consciousness that the hazards from earthquakes are very real and the potential losses very great, it seems inevitable that we shall learn the lessons of 1906 and 1989 yet again.[5]

Damage in the Marina District, San Francisco, after the Loma Prieta earthquake, 1989.

The habit of building on poor foundations in earthquake country is, needless to say, hardly unique to California or Japan. Dozens of examples from many civilizations throughout history are detailed in *Apocalypse: Earthquakes, Archaeology, and the Wrath of God* by the geophysicist Amos Nur (who himself narrowly escaped serious injury in 1989 by diving under his desk beneath crashing steel bookcases in his office at Stanford University). For instance, the millions of visitors to the Colosseum in Rome cannot avoid noticing that only part of the external wall of the famous oval amphitheatre remains standing, but they remain unaware of the reason why the northern section survived while the southern collapsed. The cause was an earthquake. A millennium after the fall of ancient Rome, the city was struck by a quake in 1349 that produced widespread damage, and even more serious damage in the Alban Hills east of the capital. In 1995 a seismic study of the foundations of the Colosseum, using sound waves to create images of the subsurface structure, revealed that the southern half of the Colosseum rests on alluvium – accumulated sediment filling the prehistoric bed of a tributary of the River Tiber that is now extinct. The northern, undamaged, half stands on the riverbank, where the ground is older and more stable.

The Colosseum, Rome, viewed from the east.

Earthquake
destruction, Van,
Turkey, 2011. More
than 6,000 houses were
completely destroyed.

Over the centuries, much has been learnt about earthquake-resistant construction by trial and error. Hence the evolution of the complicated wooden joints that support the roofs of Japanese pagodas. In Turkey and Kashmir, notes Susan Hough, 'people have long recognized creaks and cracks as an effective defence against earthquake damage', because these imperfections help to prevent a building from destructive swaying. 'Traditional architecture in these regions incorporates a patchwork quilt of wood elements and masonry infill, producing buildings that are able to dissipate shaking energy in a million little internal shifts and shimmies.'[6] At Hagia Sophia in Istanbul (the former Constantinople), the greatest of the Byzantine churches, the architect-engineers of the sixth century AD used a flexible cement to allow the walls of the building to give a little during earthquakes. They added volcanic ash or other silica-rich materials to their mortar of limestone and crushed brick. This reacted with the limestone and water and produced a calcium silicate matrix – similar to that found in modern Portland cement – that can absorb seismic energy.

Modern earthquake-resistant design involves structures with steel frames and reinforced concrete, and shear walls, that is, strong walls that prevent a building from shearing too far. A shear wall forms part of Caltech's Seismological Laboratory, constructed at Pasadena shortly after hospital buildings collapsed in the destructive San Fernando earthquake of 1971, to prevent potential future embarrassment to seismologists. A recent innovation in earthquake engineering, known as base isolation, employs rubber or lead bearings between the building and its foundation in order to prevent much of the horizontal ground motion from being transmitted into the building. In Alaska, where the Trans-Alaska Pipeline passes over the Denali fault, sections have been engineered so as to lie on skids. When a magnitude-7.9 earthquake struck in 2002, this fault moved 7 metres (23 feet), but the pipeline did not break. (Given the cost of such special engineering, however, the average pipeline is allowed to break in an earthquake, and then repaired as soon as possible.)

Designs are tested for their performance during an earthquake in one of three ways. In the first place, the likely movement of a building can be calculated from formulae based on its overall size, 'stiffness' and other structural properties. Second, a model of the building can be subjected to simulated shaking on a computer. Third, a scale model of the building can be made and physically shaken on a so-called shake table. Besides the obvious expense of the last method, it suffers from another limitation: that it may not be scale invariant. A small-scale model and a life-sized building may respond differently to the same shaking. However, there are perhaps a dozen large shake tables in use around the world – one of which, at the University of California in San Diego, has a 93-square-metre (1,000-square-foot) steel platform large enough to test a full-scale slice of a seven-storey building, with a maximum load of 2,000 tonnes.

The Trans-Alaska Pipeline passes over the Denali fault on specially engineered skids.

The Transamerica
Pyramid, San Francisco,
California, completed in
1972, was designed to
withstand shaking by a
major earthquake.

A building's natural period of oscillation – in which it would sway back and forth if you gave it a push (like a playground swing) – is important in earthquakes. The natural period of a ten-storey building is about one second, and this increases by about one second for every ten additional storeys. Skyscrapers therefore have a longer natural period than low-rise buildings. With a short period of vibration of, say, a tenth of a second in the horizontal ground shaking, an earthquake will make furniture and other objects inside a building rattle, but leave the structure unmoved. With a long period of, say, ten seconds, the whole building will move as one, without swaying significantly. But if the period of the vibration matches the natural period of the building, the two will be in resonance – like a swing pushed at just the right moment on each oscillation so as to make it go higher and higher – and the building will sway. There will be a strong likelihood of collapse if the shaking persists.

More crucial, however, to the proneness of a building to collapse is the choice of construction material, and of course the quality of construction. Reinforced concrete buildings generally survive the best in earthquakes, timber-frame buildings the next best, brick buildings fare less well than timber-frame buildings and adobe (sun-dried brick) buildings suffer the most damage – as proved by the magnitude-6.6 earthquake that struck the predominantly adobe city of Bam and its surrounding Kerman province in southeastern Iran in 2003, in which more than 26,000 lives were lost. The adobe buildings of the Middle East and South America, durable and cool inside as they are, are unable to withstand even a tenth of the acceleration due to gravity in a horizontal direction. The situation is made worse by the fact that since adobe is not strong, builders compensate by making house walls thick, which makes them heavy and, in an earthquake, lethal to their occupants.

In *Disaster Deferred*, his study of the future risks from the New Madrid seismic zone, Seth Stein illustrates this with graphs showing the percentage of collapsed buildings made of different construction materials plotted against increased earthquake intensity on the Modified Mercalli Scale. He then relates the graphs to the New Madrid earthquake of December 1811 with the following analysis. As in any earthquake, writes Stein,

> The intensity of shaking got smaller with increasing distance from the [epicentre]. New Madrid itself experienced shaking with intensity about IX. If there had been unreinforced brick buildings there, about half would have collapsed. About 20 per cent of wood-frame houses would have collapsed as well as 10 per cent of reinforced concrete buildings (which hadn't been invented yet). Farther from the earthquake, Memphis (which didn't exist yet) would have experienced shaking with intensity about VII, which would have collapsed about 5 per cent of unreinforced brick buildings, but few if any

Modified Mercalli
intensity plotted against
percentage of buildings
collapsed for different
construction materials.

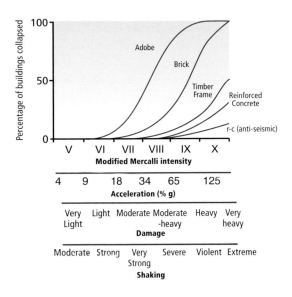

wood-frame or concrete buildings. Even farther away, the
shaking at St Louis (which did exist) was intensity VI,
and buildings didn't collapse.[7]

The point of such figures, for Stein, is to quantify honestly the
risk to the American Midwest from another severe earthquake
in the region. In his view, as the data from GPS measurements of
local plate movement become more extensive over time, the less
likely a severe earthquake in the area appears to be, and the
fewer grounds there are for the 'better safe than sorry' argument
of the US government. Its Federal Emergency Management
Agency (FEMA), supported by the USGS, has been pushing for
building codes in the Midwest to be as stringent as those in
California – despite the inevitably astronomical expense of
retrofitting, which would have to be borne by the cities in question, requiring cuts in other services. (Even in California most of
the state's hospitals do not meet the standards for retrofits, which
would require about $50 billion in total.) Stein is unconvinced
both by the risk of such a Midwest earthquake occurring and
by the proposed federal antidote. 'The reason there's been little
discussion of the costs of stringent construction standards is the

assumption that someone else will pay', he writes.[8] He calls the FEMA proposal 'an expensive cure for the wrong disease', like 'chemotherapy for a cold'.[9]

This is not to underestimate the power of what happened in a once sparsely populated area of Missouri during the three major earthquakes of 16 December 1811, 23 January 1812 and 7 February 1812. Eyewitness evidence shows that they created waterfalls in the Mississippi River and even, astonishingly, caused the flow of the river to reverse. An observer named Timothy Flint wrote:

> A bursting of the earth just below the village of New Madrid arrested this mighty stream in its course, and caused a reflux of its waves, by which in a little time a great number of boats were swept out by the ascending current into the bayou, carried out and left upon the dry earth.[10]

Jared Brooks, a resident of Louisville, Kentucky, documented – and catalogued according to his own estimate of their intensity – more than 600 separate felt earthquakes between 26 December

Mississippi riverboats during the New Madrid earthquake, Missouri, 1812.

1811 and 23 January 1812. The persistent legend that the quakes even caused the church bells of Boston to peal is untrue, as proved by the lack of any mention of the quake in contemporary newspapers in the Boston area; but they did set church bells ringing in Charleston, South Carolina, nearly 1,000 kilometres (600 miles) away from New Madrid. Their magnitude was not as great as the range 8–8.75 formerly believed; they were probably in the range 7.4–8.1, or even as low as 7.0. But, as Hough notes, the New Madrid sequence 'remains the most dramatic example of an extended earthquake sequence with multiple large mainshocks ever witnessed in the United States'.[11] Were something comparable to happen today, with the region's present population, it would probably rank as one of the greatest natural disasters ever to strike the United States.

How likely is this during the next few decades? Plate tectonic theory does not predict any major earthquakes in the middle of plates, and this is supported by the dearth of plate movement in the area as measured by GPS surveys. No major Midwestern earthquake has occurred for two centuries, unlike in the area of the San Andreas fault; instead, there have been aftershocks of low magnitude, especially during the past century. Some palaeoseismic observations of sand blows suggest that there were previous large earthquakes in 1450 and 900. The record is admittedly rather meagre compared with the San Andreas excavations at Pallett Creek in California, for lack of a surface fault to excavate in the New Madrid zone. So the answer to the '$64,000 question' seems to be that such an event is highly unlikely. California is justified in spending heavily on protecting itself against severe earthquakes; Missouri and the Midwest are not. The buildings of New Madrid are more likely to fall down from natural decay than to collapse during an earthquake. That, at least, is Stein's informed, dissenting opinion, after three or four decades of work in the field.

Back in earthquake country, such as California, many homeowners who can afford to do so will continue to retrofit their properties by bolting their houses to their foundations, rebuilding chimneys, reinforcing cripple walls (pin-ups) and installing

Seismic retrofit of a historic building in Charleston, South Carolina.

automatic shut-off valves, which in the event of a rupture of a gas line should prevent houses from going up in flames – as happened in the Great Kanto earthquake in Tokyo. Still simpler precautions, which are virtually cost-free, can make the difference between escape and injury, or worse. Heavy items, such as furniture and refrigerators, can be attached or strapped to wall studs. There is a one in three chance that an earthquake will strike when people are asleep. So it makes sense to avoid having objects adjacent to the bed that could fall on it in a mere second if the ground begins to shake.

For the rest of us, living where the ground beneath our feet is so stable we never bother to think about it, the closest we are likely to come to a real earthquake is on our television and computer screens, or in print. Yet even here in London, where I sit quietly writing about earthquakes, the streets have not always remained steady, as we have often had cause to recall in this book. Even my own flat swayed, almost imperceptibly, during that forgotten British tremor in 2008. Perhaps it is time for me to consider moving those piles of heavy earth-science books from the shelf located immediately above my bed.

EARTHQUAKE TIMELINE

This list makes no claim to be comprehensive. It includes only the most lethal, most destructive or otherwise significant earthquakes mentioned in the book, plus a few other notably severe quakes. Magnitudes are not given, since accurate magnitude figures did not become available until the mid-twentieth century.

Year	Region / Epicentre
1831 BC	Shandong, China
464 BC	Sparta, Greece
226 BC	Rhodes, Greece
AD 62 or 63	Bay of Naples / Pompeii, Italy
115	Antioch, Turkey
365	Crete
526	Antioch, Turkey
856	Corinth, Greece
1138	Aleppo, Syria
1290	Chihli, China
1531	Lisbon, Portugal
1556	Shensi, China
1692	Port Royal, Jamaica
1693	Catania, Italy
1737	Calcutta, India
1750	London, UK
1755	Lisbon, Portugal
1780	Iran
1783	Calabria, Italy
1811–12	New Madrid, Missouri, USA
1835	Concepción, Chile
1855	Edo (Tokyo), Japan
1857	Fort Tejon, California, USA
1857	Naples, Italy

1868	Hayward, California, USA
1880	Yokohama, Japan
1884	Colchester, UK
1886	Charleston, South Carolina, USA
1891	Mino-Owari, Japan
1896	Sanriku, Japan
1897	Assam, India
1906	San Francisco, California, USA
1908	Messina, Italy
1915	Avezzano, Italy
1920	Kansu, China
1923	Kanto, Japan
1933	Long Beach, California, USA
1934	Bihar, India
1935	Quetta, India
1939	Erzincan, Turkey
1944	San Juan, Argentina
1949	Gharm Oblast, Tajikistan
1950	Assam-Tibet
1960	Agadir, Morocco
1960	Southern Chile
1964	Prince William Sound, Alaska, USA
1970	Ancash, Peru
1971	San Fernando, California, USA
1972	Managua, Nicaragua
1975	Haicheng, China
1976	Guatemala
1976	Tangshan, China
1977	Vrancea, Romania
1980	El Asnam, Algeria
1980	Southern Italy
1985	Michoacan, Mexico
1988	Northern Territory, Australia
1988	Spitak, Armenia
1989	Loma Prieta, California, USA
1990	Caspian Sea, Iran
1990	Luzon, Philippines
1992	Landers, California, USA
1993	Latur, India
1994	Northridge, California, USA
1995	Kobe, Japan
1998	Papua New Guinea
1999	Izmit, Turkey
2001	Gujarat, India

2003	Bam, Iran
2004	Sumatra / Indian Ocean
2005	Kashmir, Pakistan
2008	Sichuan, China
2009	L'Aquila, Italy
2010	Port-au-Prince, Haiti
2010	Canterbury, New Zealand
2011	Christchurch, New Zealand
2011	Tohoku, Japan

REFERENCES

1 **Earth-shattering Events**

1 The three quotations are from a news report on the earthquake in *The Times* (London), 27 February 2008.

2 Thomas Short, *A General Chronological History of the Air, Weather, Seasons, Meteors, etc.* (London, 1749), vol. I, p. vi.

3 Ibid., vol. II, pp. 165 and 167.

4 Thomas Allen, *The History of the County of Lincoln* (Leeds, 1830), p. 311. In *A History of British Earthquakes* (Cambridge, 1924), Charles Davison mentions this earthquake in 1114 (p. 290), but does not include it in his 'catalogue of British earthquakes' (p. 14), on the grounds that its seismic origin is not established.

5 Letter dated 15 October 1692, in *Memoirs of John Evelyn, Esq., FRS* (London, 1827), vol. IV, p. 342.

6 *The Letters of Horace Walpole* (London, 1857), vol. II, pp. 202–3.

7 Davison, *A History of British Earthquakes*, p. 336.

8 Peter Haining, *The Great English Earthquake* (London, 1976), p. 86.

9 *Essex Telegraph*, 26 April 1884, quoted ibid., p. 184.

10 [Bureau of Social Affairs, Home Office, Japan], *The Great Earthquake of 1923 in Japan* (Tokyo, 1926), p. 137.

11 M. K. Gandhi, *Collected Works of Mahatma Gandhi* (New Delhi, 1974), vol. LVII, p. 165.

12 Akira Kurosawa, *Something Like an Autobiography*, trans. Audie E. Bock (New York, 1983), p. 50.

13 Ibid., pp. 52–4.

14 Haruki Murakami, *after the quake*, trans. Jay Rubin (London, 2002), p. 2.

15 Ibid., p. 17.

16 Charles Darwin, *The Voyage of the Beagle* [1839], ed. Janet Browne and Michael Neve (London, 1989), p. 235.

17 Public statement by Prime Minister Naoto Kan on 13 March 2011.

18 Darwin, *Voyage of the Beagle*, p. 232.

19 Amos Nur and Dawn Burgess, *Apocalypse: Earthquakes, Archaeology, and the Wrath of God* (Princeton, NJ, 2008), p. 6.

2 Lisbon, 1755: The Wrath of God

1   *Illustrated London News* (30 March 1850), p. 222.
2   Charles Dickens, 'Lisbon', *Household Words* (25 December 1858), p. 89.
3   Edward Paice, *Wrath of God: The Great Lisbon Earthquake of 1755* (London, 2008), p. xvi. Much of this chapter is indebted to Paice's book.
4   Peter Gould, 'Lisbon 1755: Enlightenment, Catastrophe, and Communication', in *Geography and Enlightenment*, ed. David N. Livingstone and Charles W. J. Withers (Chicago, IL, 1999), p. 402.
5   C. R. Boxer, *The Portuguese Seaborne Empire, 1415–1825* (London, 1977), p. 189.
6   Quoted in Paice, *Wrath of God*, p. 65.
7   Quoted ibid., p. 73.
8   Quoted ibid., pp. 115–16.
9   Quoted ibid., p. 82.
10 Charles Davison, *Great Earthquakes* (London, 1936), p. 3.
11 Quoted in Bruce A. Bolt, *Earthquakes and Geological Discovery* (New York, 1993), p. 8.
12 Quoted in Robert G. Ingram, 'Earthquakes, Religion and Public Life in Britain during the 1750s', in *The Lisbon Earthquake of 1755: Representations and Reactions*, ed. Theodore E. D. Braun and John B. Radner (Oxford, 2005), p. 115.
13 Alexander Pope, *Essay on Man*, Epistle I, lines 285–94.
14 Quoted in Paice, *Wrath of God*, p. 192.
15 Voltaire, *Candide and Other Stories*, trans. Roger Pearson (Oxford, 2006), p. 13.
16 Dickens, 'Lisbon', p. 88.

3 Seismology Begins

1   Quoted in Bryce Walker et al., *Earthquake* (Amsterdam, 1982), p. 50.
2   Robert Mallet, *Great Neapolitan Earthquake of 1857: The First Principles of Observational Seismology* (London, 1862), vol. I, p. vii.
3   Ibid., pp. 35–6.
4   James Dewey and Perry Byerly, 'The Early History of Seismometry', *Bulletin of the Seismological Society of America*, 59 (1969), p. 195.
5   Quoted in A. L. Herbert-Gustar and P. A. Nott, *John Milne: Father of Modern Seismology* (Tenterden, Kent, 1980), p. 71.

6 As advanced by Herbert-Gustar and Nott.
7 Quoted in Gregory Clancey, *Earthquake Nation: The Cultural Politics of Japanese Seismicity, 1868–1930* (Berkeley, CA, 2006), pp. 64–5.
8 Ibid., p. 101.
9 Quoted in Herbert-Gustar and Nott, *John Milne*, p. 91.
10 *San Francisco Call*, 5 August 1906.

4 Tokyo, 1923: Holocaust

1 Gregory Smits, 'Shaking Up Japan: Edo Society and the 1855 Catfish Picture Prints', *Journal of Social History*, 39 (2006), p. 1,046.
2 Ibid., p. 1,072.
3 Gregory Clancey, *Earthquake Nation: The Cultural Politics of Japanese Seismicity, 1868–1930* (Berkeley, CA, 2006), p. 218.
4 Quoted ibid., p. 218.
5 Quoted ibid., p. 220.
6 Ibid.
7 *The Age* (Melbourne), 4 September 1923.
8 Quoted in Bruce A. Bolt, *Earthquakes and Geological Discovery* (New York, 1993), p. 20.
9 Clancey, *Earthquake Nation*, p. 221.
10 Quoted in Peter Hadfield, *Sixty Seconds That Will Change the World: How the Coming Tokyo Earthquake Will Wreak Worldwide Economic Devastation*, revd edn (London, 1995), pp. 2–3.
11 Quoted ibid., p. 3.
12 Ibid., p. 5 (based on reports in the *Japan Times* during September 1923).
13 Paul Waley, *Tokyo: City of Stories* (New York and Tokyo, 1991), pp. 171–2.
14 Ryunosuke Akutagawa, *Rashomon and Other Stories*, trans. Jay Rubin (London, 2006), p. 197.
15 Quoted in Edward Seidensticker, *Tokyo Rising: The City since the Great Earthquake* (New York, 1990), p. 39.
16 Yasanuri Kawabata, *The Dancing Girl of Izu and Other Stories*, trans. J. Martin Holman (Washington, DC, 1997), pp. 105–8.
17 [Bureau of Social Affairs, Home Office, Japan], *The Great Earthquake of 1923 in Japan* (Tokyo, 1926), p. 33.
18 Hadfield, *Sixty Seconds That Will Change the World*, p. 16.
19 Seidensticker, *Tokyo Rising*, p. 99.
20 Ibid., p. 121.

5 Measuring Earthquakes

1 Quoted in Susan Hough, *Richter's Scale: Measure of an Earthquake, Measure of a Man* (Princeton, NJ, 2007), p. 89.
2 Quoted ibid., p. 102.
3 Philip L. Fradkin, *Magnitude 8: Earthquakes and Life along the San Andreas Fault* (Berkeley, CA, 1999), p. 271.
4 Bruce A. Bolt, *Earthquakes and Geological Discovery* (New York, 1993), p. 56.
5 John McPhee, *Assembling California* (New York, 1993), pp. 283–4.
6 Quoted in Bryce Walker et al., *Earthquake* (Amsterdam, 1982), p. 86.
7 Hough, *Richter's Scale*, p. 124.
8 Ibid., p. 130.
9 Roff Smith, 'The Biggest One', *Nature*, 465 (2010), p. 24.
10 Seth Stein, *Disaster Deferred: How New Science Is Changing Our View of Earthquake Hazards in the Midwest* (New York, 2010), p. 102.
11 Ibid., p. 100.
12 Quoted in Fradkin, *Magnitude 8*, p. 274.

6 Faults, Plates and Drifting Continents

1 Quoted in A. L. Herbert-Gustar and P. A. Nott, *John Milne: Father of Modern Seismology* (Tenterden, Kent, 1980), p. 52.
2 Quoted ibid., p. 58.
3 Quoted in Philip L. Fradkin, *Magnitude 8: Earthquakes and Life along the San Andreas Fault* (Berkeley, CA, 1999), pp. 96–7.
4 Quoted in Bryce Walker et al., *Earthquake* (Amsterdam, 1982), p. 112.
5 Susan Hough, *Earthshaking Science: What We Know (and Don't Know) about Earthquakes* (Princeton, NJ, 2002), p. 1.
6 Seth Stein, *Disaster Deferred: How New Science Is Changing Our View of Earthquake Hazards in the Midwest* (New York, 2010), p. 122.
7 H. H. Hess, 'History of Ocean Basins', in *Petrologic Studies: A Volume in Honor of A. F. Buddington*, ed. A.E.J. Engel, Harold L. James and B. F. Leonard (Boulder, CO, 1962), p. 599.
8 Hough, *Earthshaking Science*, p. 8.
9 Philip Kearey and Frederick J. Vine, *Global Tectonics* (Oxford, 1990), p. 65. The original article by Vine is 'Spreading of the Ocean Floor: New Evidence', *Science*, 154 (1966), pp. 1,405–15.
10 Quoted in Andrew Robinson, *Earthshock: Hurricanes, Volcanoes, Earthquakes, Tornadoes and Other Forces of Nature*, revd edn (London, 2002), p. 28.
11 Fradkin, *Magnitude 8*, p. 12.

7 **California: The Enigma of the San Andreas Fault**

1 Marc Reisner, *A Dangerous Place: California's Unsettling Fate* (London, 2003), p. 6.
2 Philip L. Fradkin, *Magnitude 8: Earthquakes and Life along the San Andreas Fault* (Berkeley, CA, 1999), p. 145.
3 Arthur Lachenbruch and A. McGarr, 'Stress and Heat Flow', in *The San Andreas Fault System: An Overview of the History, Geology, Geomorphology, Geophysics, and Seismology of the Most Well Known Plate-Tectonic Boundary in the World*, ed. Robert E. Wallace (Denver, CO, 1990), p. 261.
4 Quoted in Richard A. Kerr, 'Weak Faults: Breaking Out All Over', *Science*, 255 (1992), p. 1,210.
5 Susan Hough, *Earthshaking Science: What We Know (and Don't Know) about Earthquakes* (Princeton, NJ, 2002), p. 26.
6 Seth Stein, *Disaster Deferred: How New Science Is Changing Our View of Earthquake Hazards in the Midwest* (New York, 2010), p. 73.
7 Quoted in Andrew Robinson, *Earthshock: Hurricanes, Volcanoes, Earthquakes, Tornadoes and Other Forces of Nature*, revd edn (London, 2002), p. 66.
8 Quoted in Richard A. Kerr and Richard Stone, 'A Human Trigger for the Great Quake of Sichuan?', *Science*, 323 (2009), p. 322.
9 Quoted in Fradkin, *Magnitude 8*, p. 81.
10 Ibid., p. 235.
11 Charles Richter, *Elementary Seismology* (San Francisco, CA, 1958), p. 498.
12 Carey McWilliams, 'The Folklore of Earthquakes' in McWilliams et al., *Fool's Paradise: A Carey McWilliams Reader* (Berkeley, CA, 2001), pp. 41–2. The article was first published in *American Mercury*, 29 (1933), pp. 199–201.
13 Fradkin, *Magnitude 8*, p. 102.
14 Ibid., p. 11.

8 **Prediction of the Unpredictable**

1 Quoted in the *Los Angeles Times*, 10 August 1996.
2 Susan Hough, *Earthshaking Science: What We Know (and Don't Know) about Earthquakes* (Princeton, NJ, 2002), p. 123.
3 Vincenzo Vittorini, quoted in Stephen S. Hall, 'At Fault?', *Nature*, 477 (2011), p. 269.
4 Quoted in Susan Hough, *Predicting the Unpredictable: The Tumultuous Science of Earthquake Prediction* (Princeton, NJ, 2010), p. 80.
5 Ibid.

6 Charles Richter, *Elementary Seismology* (San Francisco, CA, 1958), pp. 386–7.
7 Quoted in Susan Hough, *Richter's Scale: Measure of an Earthquake, Measure of a Man* (Princeton, NJ, 2007), p. 265. Hough comments on these 'most damning words' from Richter that they 'were most likely meant for amateur earthquake predictors rather than his professional colleagues'.
8 Introduction to Frank Press, 'Earthquake Prediction', *Scientific American*, 232 (1975), p. 14.
9 Hough, *Predicting the Unpredictable*, p. 110.
10 Ibid., p. 126.
11 Quoted in Helmut Tributsch, *When the Snakes Awake: Animals and Earthquake Prediction* (Cambridge, MA, 1982), p. 15.
12 Seth Stein, 'Seismic Gaps and Grizzly Bears', *Nature*, 356 (1992), p. 388.
13 *New York Times*, 27 September 1990.
14 Quoted in Richard A. Kerr, 'The Lessons of Dr Browning', *Science*, 253 (1991), p. 622.
15 Quoted in Andrew Robinson, *Earthshock: Hurricanes, Volcanoes, Earthquakes, Tornadoes and Other Forces of Nature*, revd edn (London, 2002), p. 74.
16 Jacob M. Appel, 'A Comparative Seismology', *Weber*, 18 (2001), p. 92.
17 Seth Stein, *Disaster Deferred: How New Science Is Changing Our View of Earthquake Hazards in the Midwest* (New York, 2010), p. 16.
18 Quoted in Richard S. Olson, *The Politics of Earthquake Prediction* (Princeton, NJ, 1981), p. 137.
19 Quoted in Robinson, *Earthshock*, p. 75.

9 Designing against Death

1 James Palmer, *The Death of Mao: The Tangshan Earthquake and the Birth of the New China* (London, 2012), p. 127.
2 Quoted in Peter Hadfield, *Sixty Seconds That Will Change the World: How the Coming Tokyo Earthquake Will Wreak Worldwide Economic Devastation*, revd edn (London, 1995), pp. 187–8.
3 John Casper Branner, quoted in Philip L. Fradkin, *Magnitude 8: Earthquakes and Life along the San Andreas Fault* (Berkeley, CA, 1999), p. 136.
4 Quoted ibid., p. 120.
5 Thomas C. Hanks and Helmut Krawinkler, 'The 1989 Loma Prieta Earthquake and its Effects: Introduction to the Special Issue', *Bulletin of the Seismological Society of America*, 81 (1991), pp. 1,420–21.

6   Susan Hough, *Predicting the Unpredictable: The Tumultuous Science of Earthquake Prediction* (Princeton, NJ, 2010), p. 217.

7   Seth Stein, *Disaster Deferred: How New Science Is Changing Our View of Earthquake Hazards in the Midwest* (New York, 2010), pp. 225–6.

8   Ibid., p. 228.

9   Ibid., p. 234.

10 Quoted in Susan Hough, *Earthshaking Science: What We Know (and Don't Know) about Earthquakes* (Princeton, NJ, 2002), p. 67.

11 Ibid.

SELECT BIBLIOGRAPHY

Akutagawa, Ryunosuke, *Rashomon and Other Stories*, trans. Jay Rubin
    (London, 2006)
Bolt, Bruce A., *Earthquakes and Geological Discovery* (New York, 1993)
Braun, Theodore E. D., and John B. Radner, eds, *The Lisbon Earthquake
    of 1755: Representations and Reactions* (Oxford, 2005)
[Bureau of Social Affairs, Home Office, Japan], *The Great Earthquake
    of 1923 in Japan* (Tokyo, 1926)
Clancey, Gregory, *Earthquake Nation: The Cultural Politics of Japanese
    Seismicity, 1868–1930* (Berkeley, CA, 2006)
Darwin, Charles, *Voyage of the Beagle*, ed. Janet Browne and Michael
    Neve (London, 1989)
Davison, Charles, *A History of British Earthquakes* (Cambridge, 1924)
—, *Great Earthquakes* (London, 1936)
Dewey, James, and Perry Byerly, 'The Early History of Seismometry',
    Bulletin of the Seismological Society of America, 59 (1969), pp. 183–227
Fradkin, Philip L., *Magnitude 8: Earthquakes and Life along the San
    Andreas Fault* (Berkeley, CA, 1999)
Hadfield, Peter, *Sixty Seconds That Will Change the World: How the Coming
    Tokyo Earthquake Will Wreak Worldwide Economic Devastation*, revd
    edn (London, 1995)
Haining, Peter, *The Great English Earthquake* (London, 1976)
Hall, Stephen S., 'At Fault?', *Nature*, 477 (2011), pp. 264–9
Herbert-Gustar, A. L., and P. A. Nott, *John Milne: Father of Modern
    Seismology* (Tenterden, Kent, 1980)
Hough, Susan, *Earthshaking Science: What We Know (and Don't Know)
    about Earthquakes* (Princeton, NJ, 2002)
—, *Richter's Scale: Measure of an Earthquake, Measure of a Man* (Princeton,
    NJ, 2007)
—, *Predicting the Unpredictable: The Tumultuous Science of Earthquake
    Prediction* (Princeton, NJ, 2010)
Kawabata, Yasunari, *The Dancing Girl of Izu and Other Stories*, trans.

J. Martin Holman (Washington, DC, 1997)

Kearey, Philip, and Frederick J. Vine, *Global Tectonics* (Oxford, 1990)

Kerr, Richard A., 'Weak Faults: Breaking Out All Over', *Science*, 255 (1992), pp. 1,210–12

Kurosawa, Akira, *Something Like an Autobiography*, trans. Audie E. Bock, pbk edn (New York, 1983)

Mallet, Robert, *Great Neapolitan Earthquake of 1857: The First Principles of Observational Seismology*, 2 vols (London, 1862)

Murakami, Haruki, *after the quake*, trans. Jay Rubin (London, 2002)

Nur, Amos, and Dawn Burgess, *Apocalypse: Earthquakes, Archaeology, and the Wrath of God* (Princeton, NJ, 2008)

Ouwehand, C., *Namazu-e and Their Themes* (Leiden, 1964)

Paice, Edward, *Wrath of God: The Great Lisbon Earthquake of 1755* (London, 2008)

Palmer, James, *The Death of Mao: The Tangshan Earthquake and the Birth of the New China* (London, 2012)

Reisner, Marc, *A Dangerous Place: California's Unsettling Fate* (London, 2003)

Richter, Charles, *Elementary Seismology* (San Francisco, CA, 1958)

Robinson, Andrew, *Earthshock: Hurricanes, Volcanoes, Earthquakes, Tornadoes and Other Forces of Nature*, revd edn (London, 2002)

Seidensticker, Edward, *Tokyo Rising: The City since the Great Earthquake* (New York, 1990)

Smith, Roff, 'The Biggest One', *Nature*, 465 (2010), p. 24

Smits, Gregory, 'Shaking Up Japan: Edo Society and the 1855 Catfish Picture Prints', *Journal of Social History*, 39 (2006), pp. 1,045–77

Stein, Seth, *Disaster Deferred: How New Science Is Changing Our View of Earthquake Hazards in the Midwest* (New York, 2010)

Tributsch, Helmut, *When the Snakes Awake: Animals and Earthquake Prediction* (Cambridge, MA, 1982)

Voltaire, *Candide and Other Stories*, trans. Roger Pearson (Oxford, 2006)

Waley, Paul, *Tokyo: City of Stories* (New York and Tokyo, 1991)

Walker, Bryce, and the editors of Time-Life Books, *Earthquake* (Amsterdam, 1982)

Wallace, Robert E., ed., *The San Andreas Fault System: An Overview of the History, Geology, Geomorphology, Geophysics, and Seismology of the Most Well Known Plate-Tectonic Boundary in the World* (Denver, CO, 1990)

Wang, Kelin, Qi-Fu Chen, Shi-hong Sun and Andong Wang, 'Predicting the 1975 Haicheng Earthquake', *Bulletin of the Seismological Society of America*, 96 (2006), pp. 757–95

Wegener, Alfred, *The Origin of Continents and Oceans*, trans. John Biram, 4th edn (New York, 1966)

Weisenfeld, Gennifer, *Imaging Disaster: Tokyo and the Visual Culture of Japan's Great Earthquake of 1923* (Berkeley, CA, 2012)

ASSOCIATIONS AND WEBSITES

British Geological Survey
www.earthquakes.bgs.ac.uk

California Institute of Technology Seismological Laboratory
www.seismolab.caltech.edu

European-Mediterranean Seismological Centre
www.emsc-csem.org

Japan Meteorological Agency
www.jma.go.jp/en/quake

Pacific Earthquake Engineering Research Center,
University of California, Berkeley
http://nisee2.berkeley.edu

Seismological Society of America
www.seismosoc.org

United States Geological Survey
www.usgs.gov

The international science journals *Nature* and *Science*
regularly cover earthquakes and seismology
www.nature.com
www.sciencemag.org

PHOTO ACKNOWLEDGEMENTS

The author and the publishers wish to express their thanks to the following sources of illustrative material and/or permission to reproduce it:

AlexHe34: p. 143; Archive of the Alfred Wegener Institute: p. 116; The Bancroft Library: pp. 29, 112, 144 (California Historical Society); Ben+Sam: p. 160; Bigstock: p. 127 (M. Brandes); British Library, London: p. 28; © The Trustees of the British Museum: pp. 10, 36, 54; John Derr: p. 157; Getty Images: pp. 16, 172, 175; Istockphoto: p. 180 (Niko Guido); The Library of the Old Dublin Society: p. 55; The National Oceanic and Atmospheric Administration: p. 126; Rex Features: pp. 30–31, 52, 63 (Roger-Viollet), 173 (Roy Garner); © Scala, Florence: p. 60 (White Images); Daniel Schwen: p. 183; Shutterstock: pp. 6 (Shi Yali), 25 (Tim Ackroyd), 179 (SF Photo); Marie Tharp Maps: pp. 118–19; TheWiz83: p. 22; University of California, San Diego: pp. 34, 145; US Air Force: p. 25 (Master Sgt Jeremy Lock); US Geographical Survey: pp. 94 (W. L. Huber), 132, 137, 150 (James W. Dewey), 155 (R. E. Wallace), 176 (C. E. Meyer), 182; US Marine Corps: p. 26 (Lance Cpl Garry Welch).

INDEX

EARTHQUAKE

Cecchi, P. F. 63–4

Chamberlin, Rollin 117

Charleston, South Carolina 130,
187, 188
Chile 8, 17, 23, 26–7, 79, 102, 107,
109, 110, 124
China 8, 22, 29, 62, 79, 91, 123,
136, 143–4, 153–6, 163, 164
Christchurch, New Zealand 24, 25
Clancey, Gregory 78, 83
Clarke, Arthur C. 127
Cluff, Lloyd 177
Colchester, Essex 11, 41
Colosseum, London 35–7
Colosseum, Rome 179, 179
Concepción, Chile 23, 26–7
Condon, Emmet 145
continental drift 116–17
Cousin, Jean (the Elder) 17
Croyland (Crowland),
Lincolnshire 9
Czech Republic 34

dams 142–4, 143
Darwin, Charles 23, 26–7, 115
Davison, Charles 8–9, 11, 47, 112,
122
Denver, Colorado 141
Dewey, James 64
Diamond, Jared 33
Dickens, Charles 37–8, 51
Dietz, Robert 121
Dover, Kent 9
Drews, Robert 33

earthquake
intensity 54, 57, 58–9, 95, 96–7,
103
intraplate 130–1, 170
magnitude 58, 59, 69, 95, 96–8,
103–10, 104, 109
prediction 78–9, 82, 83, 152–9,
162–70, 157, 164
waves 47–8, 56, 74, 98–103,

114, 157–8, 99
Earthquake (film) 148, 149, 148
earthquakes
Alaska (1964) 109, 110, 124
Ansei (1855) 18, 19, 69, 75–8,
80, 90, 93, 19, 76, 77
Cairo (1992) 171, 172
Calabria (1783) 53–5, 111, 54
Chile (1960) 107, 109, 110, 124
Christchurch (2011) 24, 25, 25
Concepción (1835) 23, 26–7, 27
Fort Tejon (1857) 134, 135
Great English (1884) 11–12,
41, 11
Great Kanto (1923) 13–14, 18–
21, 28, 39, 40, 69, 75, 80–93, 95,
100, 134, 152, 163, 172–5, 188,
14, 81, 85, 86, 90, 91,
92, 173
Great Neapolitan (1857) 55–8,
67, 95, 111, 57
Haicheng (1975) 136, 153–6,
163
Haiti (2010) 23–4, 172, 24
Hayward (1868) 133, 144–5,
165, 177
Indian Ocean (2004) 23, 24, 29,
107, 108–9, 124
Kobe (1995) 21, 109, 174
Landers (1992) 136
L'Aquila (2009) 22–3, 153, 22
Lisbon (1755) 16, 17, 27, 35–
51, 83, 95, 98, 163, 36, 41, 42,
44, 45, 50
Loma Prieta (1989) 109, 110,
115, 135–6, 137, 138, 144, 167,
176, 177–8, 137, 178
London (1750) 9–10, 53, 10
Long Beach (1933) 94, 95–6,
146–7, 176, 94
Messina (1908) 52, 73, 79, 52
Mino-Owari (1891) 68–72, 73,
78, 69, 70–71
Mexico City (1985) 28–9